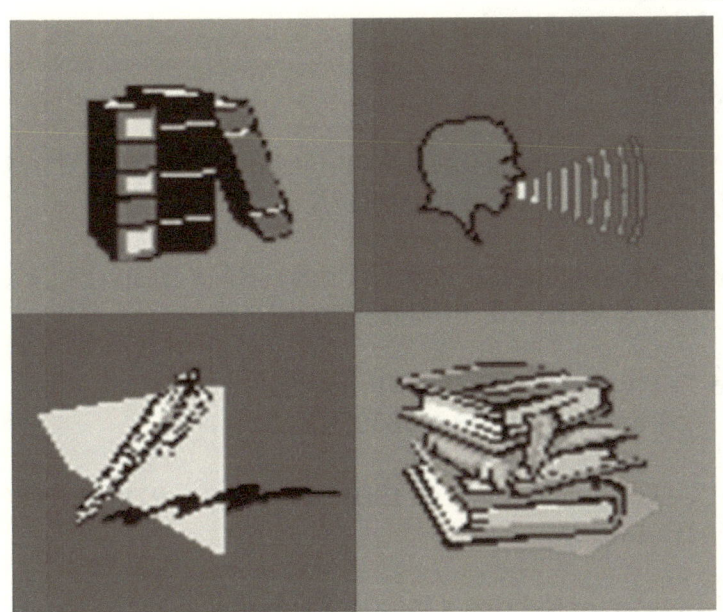

Sybrina's Phrase Thesaurus
Volume 4
Earth Views and Colors

By Sybrina Durant

Sybrina's Phrase Thesaurus Book – Earth Views and Colors

©1999 & 2013

Volume 1 - Moving Parts – Part 2 - Print ISBN # ISBN-13: 978-1481928182 & ISBN-10: 148192818X

Volume 2 - Moving Parts – Part 1 - Print ISBN # ISBN-13: 978-1480083189 & ISBN-10: 1480083186

Volume 3 - Physical Attributes – Print ISBN # ISBN-13: 978-1481983051 & ISBN-10: 1481983059

Volume 4 - Earth Views – Print ISBN # ISBN-13: 978-1481983136 & ISBN-10: 148198313X

Other ISBN #'s for Sybrina's Phrase Thesaurus
Ebook - 978-0-9729372-0-7

Contact **Sybrina@sybrina.com**

Improve your writing skills...Increase your command of the English language with Sybrina's Phrase Thesaurus. If you use a dictionary or thesaurus, you'll love this writer's aid. Tens of thousands of creative phrases...Hundreds of categories to choose from. Excellent writers aid and fun to read, too!

Have you ever hit a brick wall with your writing? Can't always get the creative juices flowing when you need them? Sybrina's Phrase Thesaurus can help you! Wish you had a better way with words? Is English a new language for you? Sybrina's Phrase Thesaurus can help you!

Sybrina's Phrase Thesaurus is a reference tool for anyone with a need to compose unique, descriptive phrases. It's a great tool for creative writers of any genre including students, people just learning English, people wanting to improve their communication skills, artistic professionals like photographers, videographers, models, actors and many others.

Anyone who enjoys reading unique descriptive phrases will love Sybrina's Phrase Thesaurus because it is packed full of descriptive phrases on every subject ...from descriptions of the body, and how it looks, moves and interacts ...to word pictures describing of all types of landscapes, waterscapes and skyscapes.

Just read the phrases and use what you want just as they're written or better yet, read all the suggested phrases in a particular category for inspiration to conquer your writer's block!

Here's how to use it. All of the categories are coded. Just use the index at the back of the book to browse the different categories. Find one you are interested in and use the code to go directly to the group of phrases for that category.

Sybrina's Phrase Thesaurus was first offered for sale, in 1993, in pdf format with a hyperlinked table of contents. The tool is still available at PhraseThesaurus.com. The book has been available, in its entirety, as an Ebook since 2009. The massive size of the book, well over 800 pages, made it financially impossible to offer it in print until the print-on-demand industry became easily available to independent authors and publishers. In order to keep the price of the books in print lower, the book has been split into 4 smaller sections.

The books are sub-titled and described as follows:

Volume 1 - MOVING PARTS – Part 1 - This book encompasses the top half of the body, describing how it moves and functions. Part 1 covers the everything to do with the head, including voluntary and involuntary actions such as listening, blushing breathing, winking, coughing, singing and much more.

Volume 2 - MOVING PARTS – Part 2 - This book encompasses all of the lower body below the neck, describing how it moves and functions. Part 2 covers topics such as shrugging shoulders, reaching out to touch someone, heart beats, shivering, aching bones, stomach churning, hand gestures, posing, sitting, walking, running and much more. The Body In Motion section includes jumping, skipping, turning, sitting down and getting up, bending, stretching, squirming, falling and body in repose. The Daily Activities section includes creative ways to describe eating meals, driving cars, using a telephone, changing clothes and more. The Figures (or Expressions) Of Speech section includes ideas for writing smooth flowing conversations. Much more than just "He said, She said". Finally the Emotions section contains descriptions of emotions. Joy, anger, fear, sadness and many more.

Volume 3 - PHYSICAL ATTRIBUTES – This book encompasses all of the body describing how different parts of the human body look, from head to toe. This book covers topics such as facial shapes and expressions, age and youth. There are descriptions for bald heads and different kinds of hair styles and colors. There are descriptions for skin colors and textures and all kinds of ways to describe eyes, ears, noses and mouths. The rest of the body is described in great detail as well.

Volume 4 - EARTH VIEWS - This book consists of Landscapes (plains, hills, mountains, valleys), Waterscapes (waterfalls, streams, rivers, ponds) and Skyscapes (morning, sunny, cloudy, rain, space, stars) and much more. There is also a section for COLORS with descriptions for all the colors in the rainbow plus other things like metals, shiney, light, dark, day and night.

Enjoy them all!

EARTH VIEWS

SS

SKYSCAPES

SS1-1 (SKYSCAPES – MORNING - SUNRISE)

1. sun clears the horizon
2. fires of sunrise
3. the sun's disc bisected the horizon
4. the rising sun only began to burn away the morning mist
5. bleak early moments of sunrise
6. wan yellow light of dawn
7. true blaze of sunrise arose above the last vestiges of night
8. umber light painted across the sky
9. it was just beginning to grow light
10. the pale light of dawn
11. the morning dawned frosty and bright
12. pale glow of the sky
13. it was mere wan lightness first
14. rosy sky spread over the eastern land
15. lustrous yellows in the east
16. a streak of morning in the eastern sky
17. the pale light in the sky where the day was coming
18. no promise of day was in the murky sky
19. red lighting of the sky
20. the eastern sky began to quicken
21. the magical lights of the horizon
22. morning rends the vaulted sky
23. cleft the night with a wavy golden edge
24. the stars seemed dying away in the brightening sky
25. drowsing earth between the day and night
26. all the eastern sky began to silver and shine
27. the gray dawn streaked the sky

28. that gloomy moment usually precedes the dawn
29. the full triumph of light over darkness
30. shone like a great rose window at the end of a cathedral aisle
31. the morning dawned pearly and lustrous
32. holy hush of silvery sky
33. a sky that was pale golden and ethereal
34. gloried over with trails of saffron and rosy cloud
35. the eastern sky was all silvery and cloudless
36. the east reddens up
37. in the early cool morning
38. wake in the soft summer mornings
39. next morning, bright and early
40. gladness of the morning
41. on a sunny September morning
42. gray morning had resolved itself
43. the kiss of the morning
44. gray and cheerless aspect that early morning gives to everything out of the sun
45. the morning got around at last
46. so early that the shaded places still smelt like night time, and the sunny spots had hardly felt the sun
47. distinct in the still morning air
48. the brightest mornings of late summer shone upon her
49. few tattered clouds of the morning enlarged and united
50. morning glared in like a specter

SS1-2 (SKYSCAPES - DAY)

1. pale blue dome of the sky
2. azure depths of the sky
3. cerulean tint of the sky
4. an azure sky fleeced with passing clouds
5. bright clean glare of day
6. the usual soft tints of the sky
7. blue and fleecy sky

8.   the sky palely blue
9.   bathed in ghostly day
10. it was a clear, cold, winter day, with snow upon the ground
11. the time of the day was right for the eclipse
12. we had a blazing sunny day
13. on a dark winter's day
14. the day was as dark as the night
15. dark, foggy days in London
16. after long and busy days
17. after a long, hard day
18. many a bitter day
19. on a certain dreadful day
20. on the horridest days
21. this day- wetter, muddier, colder
22. the days were so dark and long
23. on the evening of a winter's day
24. the exceptional few days
25. that day was an irksome time
26. the mercury of those days had a trick of falling unexpectedly
27. day began to break
28. the day glided on to its end
29. there can never have been
30. such a heavy and cold rain on a summer day
31. days, just hastening to their end
32. after a fatiguing day
33. seemed to threaten a dreary day
34. watch the approach of day
35. one wet day
36. at all hours of the day
37. in the popular creed of that day
38. on the day whose history I have been writing
39. summer days passed pleasantly
40. to the days called ancient
41. ready for the pleasures of the day

42. on a breezy, sunny day
43. a breezy, cloudless day
44. wished the sun would rise in the middle of the day
45. a lovely day succeeded
46. such a beautiful day
47. the day might remain perfect
48. the waning day had such an inviting influence
49. the spectacle of the dying lights of day playing about the crests and pinnacles of the still and solemn upper realm
50. the whole air soon grew warmer after the splendid birth of the day
51. remember this day with peculiar pleasure
52. simply follow the inclination of the day
53. an eloquent welcome to the long-lost light of day
54. recall with exultation all the days of his life
55. a calm, clear day
56. a blazing hot day that brought a persistent and persecuting thirst with it
57. a few pleasant restful days
58. as bright as day, and yet the rain was falling in torrents
59. an unoccupied day
60. a bleak day
61. a great and justly honored day
62. a day which offers a fruitful theme for thought and speech
63. a day which is worthy of the veneration in which it is held
64. getting towards the long days and the short nights
65. it was pretty broad day
66. the first streak of day begun to show
67. a most awful hot day
68. towards the middle of the day
69. because the four hours that were remaining of the day could not suffice
70. in the midst of those days set apart for triumph
71. within the limits either of a natural or an artificial day
72. it appears at the close of day

73. the sun restored the cheerful day
74. the dismal day
75. the fatal day
76. betwixt the night and day
77. three sunless days
78. the rising sun the day revealed
79. my loathsome days
80. when day declines
81. day points upward from the rosy skies
82. cutting short her odious days
83. now the rising day renews the year
84. happy day approached
85. the blissful vision of a day
86. next the rosy morn disclosed the day
87. the glaring day
88. when the setting stars are lost in day
89. on a solemn day
90. receive the rushing day
91. that auspicious day
92. my declining days
93. dispels the darkness, and the day renews
94. immortal day appears
95. the scattered streaks of dawning day
96. the new day retires
97. the stains of this dishonorable day

SS1-3 (SKYSCAPES - SUNNY)

1. sun broke between cloud lines
2. broad beam of sunlight
3. the sun overcame the mists
4. the sun came down in sheets of brilliant purple
5. blinding rain-bowed noon-day
6. absorbed ultimately by the white of the sky
7. the light of heaven

8. the brightness of the sky compensating for the darkness of the earth
9. blue and fleecy sky
10. the unwearied sun
11. sun's broad circle
12. the sky was blue and blinding
13. sun poured its torrid rays out of a cloudless sky
14. the wild sky is blazing
15. the blue sky seemed to shine like a mirror
16. the sky palely blue
17. the sun is standing in the south sky
18. sun brazened all the sky
19. the vivifying ardor of a tropical sun
20. with a glory of sunshine
21. a glory of pale virgin sunshine
22. a flood of cheery sunshine
23. the saffron sky
24. the sky was an oven
25. heat infects the sky
26. a blazing sunny day
27. on a sunny September morning
28. the sunny spots had hardly felt the sun
29. when the sunny streaks had gone upward to the roof
30. the true sunny life of Shakespeare
31. on a breezy, sunny day
32. lying at full length in a sunny spot
33. lying asleep in a sunny spot
34. on a sunny flower
35. which has thrown a cloud over her sunny countenance
36. lived in happy ignorance of any world beyond the court and its sunny roofs
37. laden with panniers of sunny fruit
38. in the sunny air
39. overlooked the broad sunny sea

40. the mirth brightening the gloom into a sunny shower of feeling
41. sat on the sunny deck
42. it was bright and sunny
43. beams like a sunny day
44. coming up from that little sunny hollow
45. built in a sunny corner
46. a day of breeze and blue, warm, sunny
47. dipped down into a sunny little open
48. clouds never darkened the sunny sky
49. in its sunny haunts
50. the sunny side of the hill
51. a bayou curling between sunny, grassy banks
52. sunny colored foliage
53. fair sunny noon
54. a sunny, sleepy corner
55. the old sunny fort
56. it was as warm and as sunny as in April
57. always presenting the sunny side of life
58. a pleasant sort of sunny sight
59. a sunny-faced youngster
60. a sunny winter morning
61. a day of sunny rest
62. they bare a sunny crown
63. a sunny dell
64. the green, sunny rampart
65. the sunny quay at Syracuse
66. laughing sunny eyes
67. the sunny rock
68. in sunny weather
69. sunny with freckles
70. strings of sunny-colored gems
71. around the sunny garden
72. over the sunny landscape
73. basking under a sunny wall

74. the sweet sunny days
75. and their sunny hair
76. a sunny look of his
77. as sunny and as private as before
78. the little sunny, slanting, rough-paved German street
79. along the sunny beach
80. like flowers by sunny brooks in May
81. a bright sunny day
82. hair is like the sunny beam
83. my sunny hour
84. in a sunny shower
85. she was by nature a sunny soul
86. great big sunny kitchen
87. a nice, fat, sunny cook
88. upon the sunny plains
89. any sunny forenoon
90. such a sunny little figure
91. the sunny street of Canterbury
92. the sunny south wall
93. the sunny shore
94. those bright sunny rays
95. the sunny smiles
96. on a sunny bank
97. calling them back from their sunny youth
98. on the sunny side of life
99. in the sunny lands of song
100. in a sunny atmosphere
101. hair lay on the pillow in its usual sunny ripples
102. upon the sunny slopes
103. life should be a little sunny and a little sad
104. wrinkled visage grew almost sunny with intelligence and joy
105. through sunny meadows
106. sunny glades
107. in the sunny skies

108. the sunny beam
109. a sunny garden flower
110. sunny poets
111. its sunny hours
112. scorching sunny ray
113. morning- sunny and exceedingly mild
114. profile against the sunny sky
115. well defined against the sunny portion of the horizon

SS1-4 (SKYSCAPES - SUNSET)

1. pale sky of nightfall
2. purpling sky
3. sunset like a sheath of flame
4. the sky began to deepen towards sunset
5. sun set into a nest of purple clouds
6. flame of sunset
7. the still-bright westering sun
8. the disc of the sun began to slide down past the horizon
9. lemon-hued expanse of the western sky
10. the setting sun sent pale streamers of purple and orange across the blue of the heavens
11. the soul stirring colors of sunset
12. deepening shadows of impending twilight
13. the sun's disc bisected the horizon
14. sun was swallowed up into the black lake of oncoming night
15. sun had begun it's slide down the sky
16. umber light painted across the sky
17. pale glow of the sky
18. beneath a violet sky
19. a sun of brass hung over the horizon
20. darkness gains upon the sky
21. glow the heavens with the last steps of day
22. soothing calm of eventide
23. rosy flood of twilight

24. the colors of the western sky
25. the magical lights of the horizon
26. the sun was getting low in the sky
27. turning the western sky to flaming copper and gold
28. the sun dipped lower and lower
29. the last remains of day-light faintly streaked the western sky
30. beneath a sky lighted up by marvelous sunsets
31. a glimpse of painted sunset sky shone
32. shone like a great rose window at the end of a cathedral aisle
33. the twilight rained down out of a dappled sky
34. sunset with a heart of fiery yellow
35. a marigold sky
36. the stainless southwest sky
37. a sky that was pale golden and ethereal
38. gloried over with trails of saffron and rosy cloud
39. an apple-green western sky
40. the eastern sky was flushed faintly pink from the reflection of the west
41. a lovely yellowish-green twilight
42. glorious dome of sunset sky
43. a couple of hours before sunset
44. before sunset tonight
45. between an Upper Mississippi sunset and the aurora borealis
46. twittering with sunset softness on the slates
47. a familiar September sunset
48. walking between the sunset and the moonrise
49. the sunset rays glanced directly upon the wet uphill road
50. how beautiful was the sunset
51. in high places it is not long from sunset to night
52. in the mellow glow of sunset
53. and crimson sunset glories
54. in the sunset, when all the lower world is palled in gloom

55. her face afire like sunset
56. such a color as tinges the clouds at sunset
57. to the realms of sunset
58. the lovely appearance of the western sky at sunset
59. catch fire with the sunset
60. through a splendid golden sunset
61. a glorious sunset behind them
62. the afternoon had waned to sunset
63. watched the sunset burn on the river
64. it was yet scarce sunset
65. emerging towards sunset
66. in the glow of sunset
67. mingles at sunset with the smell of meadowsweet
68. in the pale light of the sunset
69. painted sunset sky shone like a great rose window at the end of a cathedral aisle
70. afar into the sunset west
71. on the sunset sky
72. mellow sunset light streaming through the dark old firs
73. a magnificent sunset
74. brimmed up with ruby sunset light
75. glorious dome of sunset sky
76. gloried through with sunset and the warm splendor of it streamed down
77. in the sunset afterglow
78. in the sunset land
79. by the light of a calm golden sunset
80. the sunset sky that was like a great flower with petals of crocus and a heart of fiery yellow
81. lying in the glamour of sunset
82. through the hill-gaps sunset light shone
83. the glow of the sunset was slowly fading
84. sea runs red where the sunset reaches
85. in the changing sunset embers
86. the last red sunset glimmer

87. a patch of sunset tints, faintly red
88. the last pink flush of the sunset
89. flushes like a sunset
90. a serenity, a tranquility, a calm-sunset air
91. calm, radiant sunset
92. at that same hour of sunset
93. resemblance to the warm tints of an Italian or Grecian sunset
94. in the light of the sunset clouds
95. in all its sunset glow
96. blood-red as sunset summer clouds
97. amidst the blaze of sunset halos
98. mountaintop still held the sunset, and seemed to glow with a delicate pink
99. the failing sunset
100. the approach of sunset was so very beautiful
101. marked by myriad clouds of every sunset-color- flame, purple, pink, green, violet, and all the tints of gold
102. the wonderful smoky beauty of a sunset over London
103. sunset was not far off
104. softness of the red sunset on her face
105. the sunset peeps into
106. the splendors of a sunset
107. pass into a delicate realm of sunset
108. sunset is unlike anything that is underneath it
109. what recesses of
110. ineffable pomp and loveliness in the sunset
111. faintly tinged with the rosy sunset
112. at sunset the clouds gathered again, bringing an earlier night
113. the cold red of sunset behind winter hills
114. the chilly sunset
115. whole effect resembled a sunset
116. colored with the angry crimson of a Danby sunset
117. sunset with a solemn meaning glow

118. the sky was gold and purple like an autumn sunset
119. wind sunk at sunset to a light breeze
120. like the last glimmer of sunset
121. perfectly poised in the angry red light of the sunset
122. the low red glare of sunset
123. all the rocks around turned to fire at sunset
124. sailed into the fiery sunset
125. the glory of the sunset
126. the tawny sunset, before the rise of the moon
127. the chill beauty of an autumnal sunset was now gilding
128. after sunset, and when the horizon has quite lost its richer brilliancy
129. the half-dead sunset

SS1-5 (SKYSCAPES - NIGHT)

1. the moon put in a brief appearance from behind the clouds
2. stars beginning to twinkle in the clear sky
3. stars peeping in and out of the half-overcast sky
4. bright stars displayed like jewels
5. the black velvet cloth of space
6. star flecked dark
7. starry blackness of space
8. pitch dark
9. the blackish purpling sky
10. star-speckled sky
11. a mighty canopy of coldly luminescent stars
12. black as pitch
13. tiny pinpoints of silver pierced the blackness of the sky
14. glitter of stars above
15. the broad swath of the Milky Way like an untidy scarf of samite dragged across the midnight velvet of the sky
16. a fine starlit sky lit the dark
17. Heavenly sky
18. rich indigo hue of a midnight sky

19. darkness gains upon the sky
20. a remote part of the pale night sky
21. night sky is a black dome with tiny sparks
22. night sky is a black wall
23. the cold black of the night sky
24. night with sable wings
25. the pale-colored evening sky
26. melting with the moonlit sky
27. in the sleeping sky
28. darkness is piled upon darkness
29. night trailed her robe of jewels
30. a commencement of night
31. calm loveliness of the midnight sky
32. the air was full of a purple twilight
33. calm loveliness of the midnight sky
34. the pale evening sky
35. the deep tranquility of the night
36. the sky was darkening up
37. the nocturnal sky
38. on such a bitter night
39. in the dead silence of the night
40. upon the bleak, dark night
41. slept through a whole day and far into another night
42. if night had beaten off bright day
43. a night of unbroken rest
44. one dear night when I was going to bed
45. upon a winter's night
46. in the thick gloom of darkest night
47. night is waning fast
48. let this darkness proceed, and spread night in the world
49. sweep away this creeping night
50. to feel the cold uncanny night breezes fan through the place
51. fountain of fire that turned night to noonday
52. came masked by night

53. on her bridal night
54. a starless black night
55. and rolled away into the night
56. a great night, an immense night
57. a beautiful night
58. sweep night out of the earth
59. the usual night sounds of the country
60. the whir of night birds, the buzzing of insects, the barking of distant dogs
61. the night shut down so black
62. in the night wind
63. where the day was as dark as the night
64. while the night was passing
65. one of the rare nights
66. at night when everything was so still
67. a hideous damp night
68. with the cold night outside
69. for just that one awful night
70. at dead of night
71. spending sleepless nights
72. an atmosphere like the twilight of a night vision
73. now that night had begun to fall
74. the general dark body of the night landscape
75. that blusterous night
76. a hot and still August night
77. smelt like night time
78. night spread over the sea
79. it was a cloudy night; and the light of the moon, softened and dispersed by its misty veil, was distributed over the land in pale gray
80. evening grew dark and night came on
81. on a stormy night
82. in the darkness of night
83. it is not long from sunset to night
84. dusk being in a measure banished

85. musing on all the occurrences of the night
86. at the dead of night
87. until the remnant of the night was gone
88. a summer night
89. one stormy night
90. the beautiful, refreshing, still nights of spring, when the moon pours silver light over the country
91. as the night shut down
92. one or two faint stars blinking through rifts in the night
93. out into the cold clear night
94. not a sound disturbed the deep tranquility of the night
95. during that fearful night
96. night was coming on, the darkness began to gather
97. the moonlight of peaceful winter nights
98. on a bitterly cold night
99. in the frosty night
100. the long days and the short nights
101. the night was about done
102. that still night
103. and the night clouded up and got hot
104. the night got gray, and rather thick
105. in the compass of a night
106. has the appearance of a summer's night
107. in shades of night
108. in dead of night
109. and fatal night befell
110. the silent night
111. gloomy shades of night
112. wanting to conclude the night
113. starless nights
114. hid in dusky shades of night
115. the sun withdrawn his radiant light
116. pass the tedious night
117. in endless night
118. when day declines, and feasts renew the night

119. while night obscures the skies
120. in endless night
121. vanish with the night
122. impenetrable night
123. the regions of the night
124. this eternal night
125. the realm of night

SS1-6 (SKYSCAPES – CLOUDS)

1.   clouds drifted overhead like steam from geysers
2.   small clouds, delicate and pale against the sky
3.   gray of the purest melancholy
4.   sun broke between cloud lines
5.   clean-cut white clouds
6.   the moon put in a brief appearance from behind the clouds
7.   the sun was out of sight
8.   stars peeping in and out of the half-overcast sky
9.   small clouds, delicate and pale
10.   the sky was gloomy
11.   a few fluffy white clouds
12.   an azure sky fleeced with passing clouds
13.   clouds creeping along under the sky
14.   little pink clouds
15.   an oblong piece of dull grey sky
16.   grey of the purest melancholy
17.   a dense bank of clouds
18.   soft billowing mounds of clouds
19.   clouds were undulating gently in a breeze
20.   dark-blue fragments of cloud upon an orange-yellow sky
21.   sky was covered more closely than ever with dense leaden clouds
22.   the tempests of the sky
23.   livery in dashes upon the thin airy clouds
24.   blue and fleecy sky

25. heavy clouds scudded across the sky
26. through the dizzy sky
27. clouds are broken in the sky
28. thick clouds shut in the heated air
29. heavy whiffs of white cloud
30. heavily moving masses of cloud
31. white cloud, smoke-colored at the edges
32. silver clouds against the deep blue sky
33. a white summer cloud in the blue sky
34. great black clouds came sweeping across the sky
35. covers but not hides the sky
36. the few small clouds aloft were burdened with radiance
37. little curling crests of cloud
38. covered with white streaks of cloud
39. mother-of-pearl shell of white fleecy cloudlets
40. holes for the stars to shine through
41. a great blue sky all curdled over with fluffy little white clouds
42. the sky over the firs was dark with moody clouds
43. presently the sky became overcast
44. low-hung blanket of sable cloud
45. fleeting glimpses of sky
46. cloud the sky
47. see the dingy cloud come drooping down, obscuring everything
48. watched that distant cloud spread and blacken
49. a small cloud of aromatic smoke
50. tumble up in clouds
51. out of sight among the clouds
52. moved in a cloud of its own making
53. vast clouds of radiant smoke aloft
54. the thick cloud begin to roll up and smother the tree
55. cloud seemed to pass over it and put out the light
56. little pink clouds float about
57. the piles of red or gold clouds in the west

58. purple clouds edged with dazzling brightness
59. the little fleecy, floating clouds
60. clouds tinged with rose-color and looking like flights of pink doves scurrying across the blue in a great hurry if there was a wind
61. the clouds melting or drifting or waiting softly to be changed pink or crimson or snow-white or purple or pale dove-gray
62. clouds hung low over the skylight and were either gray or mud-color, or dropping heavy rain
63. clouds, delicate and pale, creeping along under the sky southward
64. dark-blue fragments of cloud upon an orange-yellow sky
65. a large cloud, that had been hanging in the north like a black fleece, came and placed itself between her and the sun
66. few tattered clouds of the morning
67. the sun withdrew behind the clouds to emerge no more that day
68. a large lurid cloud, palpably a reservoir of rain
69. cloud was seen to be advancing overhead from the north
70. watching the rise of the cloud
71. the merest troublous cloud
72. without heeding the attack of the clouds
73. a huge bank of livid cloud with golden edges
74. dense leaden clouds
75. clouds have completely cleared
76. the thin airy clouds
77. sun shone low under the rim of a thick hard cloud
78. a flying cloud
79. in the drifting clouds
80. a smoky fog of clouds covered the whole region densely
81. the great cloud-barred disk of the sun
82. through rifts in a black cloud-bank above the sun

83. the clouds, which had for some time assumed a threatening appearance,
84. suddenly dropped
85. a huge mass of clouds, driving toward us from the north, poured down a deluge
86. the clouds by this time seemed to have done their worst
87. a vast black cloud-bank in front of us dissolved away
88. behind that low-hung blanket of sable cloud
89. the trailing fringes of the cloud-rack
90. a few wandering shreds and films of cloud moving in a lazy procession
91. draped in a cable pall of clouds
92. hidden in thick clouds which now and then dissolved to cobweb films
93. vast wreaths of white cloud
94. cloud which strung slowly out and streamed away slantwise toward the sun
95. a twenty-mile stretch of rolling and tumbling
96. vapor
97. thick smokelike cloud which feathered off
98. some white clouds which were so delicate as to almost resemble gossamer
99. webs
100. shimmering over that air film of white cloud
101. a fabric dainty enough to clothe an angel with
102. in sable thunder-clouds
103. softly gliding blots, the shadows flung from drifting clouds
104. a cloud closed around them and hid them from view
105. enveloped in clouds
106. the clouds that lowered over our housetops
107. the gathering clouds obscure the skies
108. swelling cloud hung hovering
109. gusts of weather from that gathering cloud
110. dusky clouds

111. aloft a golden cloud
112. from a breaking cloud
113. rolling clouds
114. bellowing clouds burst with a stormy sound
115. the clouds dispel
116. in a hollow cloud
117. clouds of clashing darts obscure the sky
118. cloud of dust obscured the air
119. gate of clouds
120. the clouds, driven together, resound with a crash
121. such a color as tinges the clouds at sunset or at dawn
122. the last cloud of an expiring storm
123. thick clouds shut in the heated air
124. spread the heaven with clouds
125. enveloped the whole face of heaven with a dark cloud
126. brushed away the clouds from before the face of the sun
127. vapors rose in the air and formed clouds
128. rich clouds for canopies
129. dewy clouds which cool and refresh
130. vast whirlings of swift cloud
131. heavily moving masses of cloud

SS1-7 (SKYSCAPES - SHADE)

1. the sun threw long shadows across the grass
2. the sun cast ever-shifting and slowly lengthening dappled patterns of shadow over
3. deepening shadows of impending twilight
4. casting black blots of shade
5. far off in the shade of a tree
6. a deep rose-colored shade
7. unrelieved shades of gray
8. in the cool shade
9. the spotty lights and shades from the shining moon

10. the shade which enveloped and rendered invisible the delicate gradations
11. the channel of the path was enough to throw shade
12. watching the checkered lights and shades on the tree-trunks
13. fell a heavy jagged shade over half the roadway
14. the evening shades should sufficiently screen him
15. lost in the shade
16. everything in the shade is rich and misty blue
17. the sun had now resigned to the shade
18. as adding shade to shadow
19. the dusky shades thickened
20. saw the shade leave the shady places
21. the restful quiet and shade of the forest solitudes
22. dimmed with purple shade
23. in the shade of noble woods
24. in the pleasant shade of forest trees
25. the relief of shade
26. laid there in the grass and the cool shade
27. gloomy shades of night
28. beneath a pleasing shade
29. the mystic shade
30. hid in dusky shades
31. humid shades
32. shade descended from the skies
33. the trembling shades
34. dreary shades
35. obscure in shades
36. darkness of the shades
37. the shelter of the friendly shades
38. shelter from the burning rays of the sun in the deep shade of its spreading branches
39. enjoying the cool shade of my foliage
40. the thickest shades of the wood
41. shade such as shepherds love

42. wander unavenged among the shades
43. in twilight shade of tangled thickets
44. to the realm of shades
45. rising through the mellow shade
46. as the evening shades prevail
47. the low modest shade
48. languished in the damp shade
49. shades to quench that beam of heaven
50. where trees threw up their shade from unseen trunks
51. in the matted shade
52. into the fresh, dewy shade
53. lay down in the shade of a birch
54. angling in the shade of a willow tree
55. in the dense, cool shade of the young aspens
56. unsheltered by any shade
57. where the flowers that loved the shade flourished
58. wild cherry trees along the lane put on the loveliest shades of dark red and bronzy green
59. refresh themselves in the shade
60. the lighter shades now announced the approach of day
61. transition was so sudden, without shade, without gradation of light
62. an aspect of light and shade, where the bright blaze struggled with the black night
63. under the shade of melancholy boughs
64. creatures of the shade
65. 116 degrees in the shade
66. there was a seduction in its shade
67. the lure of shade
68. twinkling through the shade
69. threw its shades half in the water, half on the land
70. in the sleepy shade and sweet air
71. in a shade that became exceedingly grateful as the day advanced
72. studied the distribution of light and shade, and its effects

73. the shade invites us to stay and rest
74. fog still hung about and screened us with its friendly shade
75. the benefit in summer of cooling shades
76. till the shades of evening enveloped every object
77. gentle and beneficial shade
78. a country of
79. almost unbroken shade
80. the shade became sunlight and the sunlight became shade again
81. walked into the mild shades about the garden
82. the shade retreated
83. trees afforded a cool and grateful shade
84. shade afforded the most charming and voluptuous retreats

SS1-8 (SKYSCAPES - RAIN)

1. a steel gray sky
2. storm subsided into a lingering mist
3. the sky was gloomy
4. sky was covered more closely than ever with dense leaden clouds
5. warm grey of quickening sky
6. the whole sky overhead seemed trembling
7. a steel sky
8. grey heavy sky
9. the wan, watery sky
10. the low, dirty sky
11. the sky was a pit of bale and dread
12. the sky was a tatter of gray
13. the sky seemed a grey mantle
14. sky seemed to suffer
15. there was a little gray in the sky
16. it began to darken up and look like rain
17. the sky was darkening up

18. while the rain beat upon the windows
19. first heavy drops of rain were falling
20. the wilder the rain lashed around, the colder and colder it got
21. the rain poured down in a deluge
22. if it rains, the drops patter and patter as if they were saying something nice
23. the pattering of the rain upon the slates and the skylight
24. thundercloud began to shed some heavy drops of rain
25. few drops of rain fell, then a sudden shower
26. rain increased and persecuted him with an exceptional persistency
27. no downward rain ever had such a torturing effect
28. rain came with such velocity that it stuck into his flesh like cold needles
29. glistening with rain
30. the rain again increased its volume
31. rain had by this time again abated
32. drizzling rain descended upon London
33. rain formed a humid and dreary halo over every well-lighted street
34. the soft touch of the dribbling rain
35. the soothing patter of the rain against the balcony windows
36. the rain poured down in torrents
37. the drenching summer rain
38. the rattling patter of the rain
39. it rained in dead earnest
40. the rain, which had nearly ceased, began again
41. rain continued to pour
42. paths which the rains had guttered
43. recent flooding rains had washed the road clear away
44. a fine, cold rain had begun to fall
45. the rain poured down in a solid sheet
46. the buzzing of the rain

47. when clouds are black with rain
48. a great storm of rain, accompanied with thunder and darkness
49. there fell a most violent storm of rain, accompanied with lightning and whirlwinds
50. the rain drove hard against the windows
51. the rain beat insistently
52. fine rain fell continuously
53. heavy and repeated showers of rain
54. clouds overshadowed the heavens and burst forth with a deluge of rain
55. the autumnal rains descended in torrents
56. a tempest of wintry rain was beating on the roof
57. there was a heavy fall of rain
58. streaming rain had already flung its white veil over all the distant forest
59. wet of the rain spurting up in tiny drops
60. the thick veil of rain
61. swollen by continuous rains
62. just as the first heavy drops of rain fell
63. for the best part of an hour the rain came merrily down
64. a fine, steady rain was falling
65. storm of rain and wind descended upon them
66. the sun shone again between light sprinkles of rain
67. scent of the fields after the rain was delicious
68. drenched with silver rain
69. a shower of golden rain
70. the tinkle of summer-rain
71. a heavy shower of rain came falling from the clouds
72. by the washing of the rains
73. brown with rain stains and time
74. soft from recent rains
75. by a pool of clear water of the rains
76. the clouds gather for the rains
77. the rain from heaven was restrained

78. blows rain down as thick as hail
79. the rustle and whisper of a fine rain falling amid the foliage
80. a cloud heavy with rain
81. the shedding of rain from a black cloud
82. when rain falls to gladden the earth
83. the rain streamed down in bucketfuls
84. rain lashed
85. a heavy rain
86. fell during the night and the next morning
87. the reckless rain
88. the wild processionals of rain
89. monotone of the rain is beautiful
90. the peace of a long warm rain
91. in the cold slow rain
92. as thick as driving rain
93. descends in a rain as fine as dust
94. watching the rain-torrents dance upon the empty pavements
95. the rain fell in quivering sheets
96. rain came down like a waterfall
97. drops of rain flew in
98. soaked with a night's rain
99. a single night of excessive rain washed away the earth
100. a dull sky, threatening rain
101. sweeping gusts of rain came up before this storm, like showers of steel
102. the dull rain fell in slanting lines
103. the cold November rain
104. a violent storm of wind and rain came on, with thunder and lightning
105. clears the air as rain does
106. rain streamed down

SS1-9 (SKYSCAPES - LIGHTENING)

1. a flash of violet lightening crossed the sky
2. jagged flash of lightening
3. lightening flitted through the sky
4. flicker of lightening crossing the sky
5. lightening in a clear sky
6. the sky had the appearance of being overcharged
7. along the dangerous sky
8. forky lightning flashed along the sky
9. the sky was a pit of bale and dread
10. an enormous lightening
11. the low lightening cast was tremulous
12. flashes of lightening
13. the lightning began to wink fitfully
14. lightning came quick and sharp now, and the place was alternately noonday and midnight
15. the lightning flashes out of a cloud
16. lightning from a clear sky
17. a faint show of lightning
18. the lightning glared out
19. by the blaze of the lightning
20. watched the silent lightning do its awful work
21. as quick as lightning
22. with lightning rapidity
23. a lightning peck
24. flee from one spot to another, like the lightning
25. soft sheet lightning expanded from a cloud, enkindling their faces
26. lightening shining over the water, and, for a moment, showing the horizon as a keen line
27. like a box of matches struck by lightning
28. where the lightning was going to strike next
29. let loose the lightning
30. whose glance flashes lightning
31. the thunder and lightning ripping around

32. quick as lightning
33. with a power of thunder and lightning
34. the lightning showed her very distinct
35. the lightning kept whimpering, and by-and-by a flash showed
36. lightning begun to flicker out
37. the heat lightning was squirting around, low down in the sky
38. lightning was glaring and flittering around so constant
39. lightning beginning to wink and flitter
40. the lightning come brisker and brisker
41. by the flicker of the lightning
42. the lightning let go a perfect sluice of white glare
43. lightning fell upon the altar, set the wood on fire
44. the forky lightning flies
45. inlaid gold of the hue of the lightning
46. shattered by a stroke of lightning
47. as swift as lightning penetrating the heights of heaven
48. quick lightning scored its trunk
49. there was a flash of red lightning
50. set in a blaze by lightning
51. a black cloud, seamed with lightning-flashes
52. wholly consumed by a stroke of lightning
53. never were lightning flashes more frequent
54. scarlet lightning that shot its fiery lances
55. a violent storm of thunder and lightning
56. now and again a bolt of lightning shot across it
57. blinding glare of lightning
58. lightning flashed as if the heavens were being cracked open
59. drawing lightning from the clouds
60. delivered by a flash of lightning
61. blasted by the lightning flash
62. lightning making rapiers of the rain

63. killed one cloudless afternoon long ago by summer lightning
64. lightning splits it
65. the appearance of a flash of lightning
66. golden flash of the lightning
67. lightning, darting this way and that way
68. flashed through the blackness like to lightning from a thundercloud
69. with the swiftness of lightning
70. sudden as lightning flashing from east to west
71. the low lightening cast was tremulous
72. scathed with lightning
73. lightning, the dazzling flame
74. the lightning shot forth
75. shone like lightning
76. there were flashes of lightning every minute and each flash lasted while one
77. could count five
78. a kind flash of lightning came from heaven and burnt them down
79. lightning might assail
80. endless lightning in the skies
81. the sea for some distance could be seen in the glare of the lightning
82. gleams of lightning shot forth
83. there came a bluish dazzling flash of lightning
84. a lighting up as if of the sun itself
85. an ill-omened flash of lightning
86. the electric matter with that of lightning
87. an angry lightning
88. vivid lightning
89. lightning-swift
90. darting like lightning
91. the brisk lightning
92. have seen in the sky a chain of summer lightning

93. the lightning spurting like water from a sluice
94. the lightning crackling overhead
95. lightning works instantaneously
96. lightning now was the color of silver, and gleamed in the heavens like a mailed army

SS1-10 (SKYSCAPES - CLEAR)

1. stars beginning to twinkle in the clear sky
2. the cerulean void
3. sky was brilliantly clear
4. a fine starlit sky lit the dark
5. the sky had again cleared
6. sky and boundless atmosphere
7. the blue sky bends over all
8. in an open patch of sky
9. a circular rift of clear sky
10. sky seems transparent
11. through the dizzy sky
12. an impenetrable screen of purest sky
13. presently the sky became clear
14. after the shower the sky became bright
15. in the abyss of brightness
16. the sky was blue and blinding
17. the sky was flushed with a wide flood of clear color
18. the sky was already a pale blue
19. the sky was the clearness of crystal
20. in the midst of an unclouded sky
21. the cloudless azure of a southern sky
22. sun poured its torrid rays out of a cloudless sky
23. the wild sky is blazing
24. the sky a blighting blue
25. the blue sky seemed to shine like a mirror
26. a settled sky
27. distinct and clear as ever

28. it was a clear, cold, winter day, with snow upon the ground
29. no fog, no mist; clear, bright, jovial, stirring, cold
30. from a clear sky
31. in clear air
32. where all had previously been so clear
33. sun is clear above the horizon
34. into the clear sky
35. glanced out into the cold clear night
36. tolerably clear weather
37. radiance was strong and clear
38. strongly marked against the clear blue sky
39. a calm, clear day
40. the day was fine and clear
41. sun rose clear this morning
42. clear and steady light
43. shines clear as day
44. as the morning wind blows clear the east
45. presently the sky became clear
46. after the shower had ceased, the sky became clear
47. in a clear night
48. calm, clear night
49. bathed in bright, clear sunshine
50. how clear and lucid
51. cold as ice and clear as crystal
52. a clear and glorious day
53. straight and clear as a ray of light
54. a clear and striking point of light
55. perfectly simple and clear
56. is clear and pure
57. very clear and definite
58. peculiarly clear
59. sun had set some time since, but the landscape was still clear in the mellow after light
60. wonderful clear icy-cold spring

61. night was clear and frosty
62. clear, echoing twilight
63. filled with a clear violet dusk
64. a clear-blue cloudless sky
65. the clear sky beyond the dark
66. clear as crystal
67. clear and bright and true
68. gloomed up in the clear blue sky
69. under the clear sky
70. the night so clear without any clouds
71. weather was clear, and slightly chilly
72. day was clear and carried the gaze out as far as the blue sky went
73. a clear sunshine evaporating the dew
74. clear in the cool September morn
75. yielding to the summons of a bright, clear day
76. all as clear as daylight
77. clear, crisp, and sparkling with stars
78. was only of clear days like those good fortune was sending
79. at last a clear light, a burst of sunshine
80. in the sky- clear, fair, inviting
81. by light, splendid and clear shines
82. by clear shining after rain
83. clear as the sun
84. like a clear heat
85. appears measurably clear
86. the air is bright and clear
87. a clear day in which to make my observations
88. the day had begun to lighten the sky and clear away the shadows
89. one clear, warm, moonlight night in September
90. what sunshine, how clear the sky is
91. the gifts of God, the clear sky, the pure air
92. exceptionally clear

93. a still, clear day, with a slight frost
94. clear as a crystal diamond reflecting the light
95. no clouds gathered in the skies
96. becomes clear and exceeding bright
97. in the starlight clear and cold
98. the broad clear orb of the sun
99. in the clear healthful air
100. pierce the clear blue skies
101. clear by-and-by
102. very clear and neat
103. ghastly clear
104. more bright than clear
105. vividly clear
106. the beginning of the holidays, and a warm, clear summer's day
107. clear, strong, and glowing
108. it is exceedingly clear

SS1-11 (SKYSCAPES - WINDY)

1. roll of big winds
2. clouds were undulating gently in a breeze
3. vagrant breezes
4. through the dizzy sky
5. no wind that blew was bitterer
6. on the wings of the wind
7. rose above the howling of the wind
8. born of the wind
9. listening to the moaning of the wind
10. wind roared about the eaves and corners
11. at last the wind sprang up and a cloud appeared
12. the gusts of wind were flaring the torches and making the shadows swash
13. about

14. the stronger the wind blew, and the wilder the rain lashed around, the colder and colder it got
15. wind rolled down
16. a little shiver of wind
17. swished about a little in the night wind
18. and when the soft wind blows over them it wafts the scent of them into the air
19. the frothy wind
20. everybody always breathes it, because the soft wind is always blowing
21. pushing along in the teeth of the wind
22. the wind howled over the roof among the chimneys like something which wailed aloud
23. trying to hold her hat on when the wind was blowing
24. the wind seemed trying to drag her thin jacket from her
25. who ever heard of wind stopping a man from doing his business
26. wind prevailed with but little abatement from its daytime boisterousness
27. went away into the wind, being caught by a gust
28. wind had freshened his warm complexion as it freshens the glow of a brand
29. ascended that magnificent climax of the wind
30. in a brisk wind
31. wind strikes the rock, runs up it, rises like a fountain to a height far above our heads, curls over us in an arch, and disperses behind us
32. a little backward current
33. wind was strong here and it tugged at his coat and lifted it
34. the wind lifting his moustache, scudding up his cheeks, under his eyelids, and into his eyes
35. voice of the wind in his ears rising and falling as it mauled and thrust him hard or softly
36. rain and wind pierce you through
37. seized by the wind

38. written only on wind
39. cold wind and a pale mist descended upon the sea
40. wind seemed to threaten a dreary day
41. the wind has increased her color
42. the increase of wind rendered promenading difficult
43. hearing the strange voice of the restless wind
44. the wind blew in a changed spirit
45. blinking weakly against the gusts of wind
46. the cold winter wind had brought with it clouds so somber, and a rain
47. so penetrating
48. wind howling in the grove
49. muffled by a rush of wind
50. russet leaves, swept by past winds in heaps
51. heard a wild wind rushing amongst trees
52. rain, wind, and darkness filled the air
53. hear the wind rave in furious gusts
54. a keen north-east wind, whistling through the crevices
55. the disconsolate moan of the wind outside
56. the frosty wind fluttered
57. swept from the sky by a rising wind
58. wild wind whirls away
59. only the faintest waft of wind roaming fitful among the trees
60. west wind whispered in the ivy
61. a wet and windy afternoon
62. the wind blew tempestuously
63. waft of wind came sweeping down and trembled through the boughs of the chestnut
64. wind roared high
65. the wind, which had shifted to the west
66. wind fresh from Europe blew over the ocean and rushed through the open casement
67. listened to the sobbing wind

68. the night-wind swept over the hill and died moaning in the distance
69. all grown aslant under the stress of mountain winds
70. wind sighed low in the firs
71. wind blew with extraordinary violence
72. with a sudden change of wind and a new moon there came a change of weather
73. floated about with the oscillation produced by wind
74. the wind appeared to soften down as if to take breath for a renewed attack
75. wandering at the mercy of wind
76. windy, whispering, moonless night
77. outdoor wind that made the deep murmurs
78. wind blows down upon my head unmercifully and gives me the ear ache
79. the scolding winds
80. cloudy evening with wind- which indeed was very seldom absent in this
81. elevated place
82. wind is so loud that you can hardly hear anything
83. cruel, cold, and biting winds
84. bitter winds came raging
85. as if a storm of wind were driving them
86. spring winds were blowing

SS1-12 (SKYSCAPES - SPACE)

1. the black velvet cloth of space
2. starry blackness of space
3. the star-scape dopplered into a smear of blue
4. the cerulean void
5. spot of outer sky
6. the vast ethereal sky
7. spacious firmament on high

8.   spangled heavens
9.   sky looked ever so deep
10.   into the measureless dim vacancies of space
11.   the whole twilight space
12.   round the space of heaven the radiant sun
13.   the empty realm of space
14.   earth, air, and seas through empty space would roll
15.   around the space of earth, and seas, and skies
16.   drives the racking clouds along the liquid space
17.   in icy space
18.   in the measureless space
19.   space…star-sprinkled and void place
20.   the whole region of space that divides earth from heaven
21.   the plains of space
22.   the realms of boundless space
23.   whirling through empty space with the phantoms
24.   the transparent deeps of space
25.   earth, satellite of a star speeding through space
26.   the twin realms of space and time
27.   crystal space
28.   in the void of space
29.   infinite corridors of space lit by ghastly suns
30.   out into the endless space, among stars and planets
31.   space, where the heavenly bodies are bound together by
       the rays that pass from star to star
32.   an infinite space equal to a finite
33.   all the way to the limits of space
34.   the stars began to crumble and a cloud of fine stardust fell
       through space
35.   a million miles broad, extending to remotest space
36.   the immeasurable background of space
37.   in the pale space of sky
38.   a great space beyond the region of the stars
39.   from the depths of cloudy space
40.   through abysmal space

41. the great space of sky
42. the star-sown vague of Space
43. the awful silences of space
44. the space beyond the suns
45. the utter solitude of space
46. from the clear space of ether
47. the cold and silence of outer space
48. the widening wastes of space
49. across the abysses of space
50. jewels glittering in the wastes of space
51. the splendor of the space
52. minute portions of celestial space

SS1-13 (SKYSCAPES - MOON)

1. the moon's riding in a ring tonight
2. the moony sky
3. melting with the moonlit sky
4. moon rode high in the naked sky
5. a young new moon
6. the spotty lights and shades from the shining moon
7. the modest light of the moon
8. with the dropping of the sun a nearly full moon had begun to raise itself
9. light of the moon was softened and dispersed by the rain
10. moonlight was distributed over the land in pale gray
11. mellow bars of moonlight
12. the glare of the moon
13. moon shed her silvery light over the whole country
14. the rain cleared away and the moon came out
15. moon lifted away the shadows
16. moonlight softly enriching it
17. the moonlight of peaceful winter nights
18. see the moon go off watch and the darkness begin to blanket the river

19. moon, which was then at full and high in the heavens,
20. moon grew dark, and by degrees losing her light, passed through various colors, and at length was totally eclipsed
21. various labors of the wandering moon
22. moon's doubtful and malignant light
23. moon's uncertain light
24. the moon shined clear
25. just as the moon is wont to relinquish her luster at the rising of the sun
26. it was sufficiently light, for the moon shone
27. in April's ivory moonlight
28. the earth beginning to glow, and the moon preparing to retire
29. before the moon shall have twice rounded her orb
30. see the moon change her shape and her hour
31. the dawn of a moonlit night
32. radiance of silver fire
33. glittering in a shaft of moonlight
34. a magnificent moon night
35. on the moon-flooded snow
36. full moon rose high into the sky, lighting the land till it lay bathed in ghostly day
37. where the moonlight streamed
38. poured in a silvery flood
39. through the pale moonlight or glimmering borealis
40. when the moon gets up and night comes
41. the crescent moon, high over the green, from a sky of crimson shone
42. while the moon, with pale and virgin luster, ornamented the canopy of heaven with silver
43. above the full and brimming moon
44. the vitreous pour of the full moon just tinged with blue
45. saw the full moon in the west grow pale and disappear in the morning light

46. that yellow half-moon late-risen and swollen as if with tears
47. low hangs the moon, it rose late
48. under that lagging, yellow, waning moon
49. the moon drooping upon the sea
50. when the moon had lifted up her beams
51. round and jolly as the harvest moon
52. the moonlight burst forth as bright as day
53. the moon presented its luminous disk
54. a ray of moonlight crossing the high window, suddenly lighted up his pale face
55. dusky white in the light of the rising moon
56. moon was an evil genius on this plain
57. the moon retained her whiteness
58. the moon still near the horizon, cut large prisms of light and shade in the streets
59. the moon, being very low, and just upon setting, cast the shadows a long way
60. great splendor of the full moon
61. as silvery as the moon
62. the rising of the sea towards the moon
63. moon that lamps the night
64. the cold beams of the moon
65. looking at the brightly shining moon
66. looked with fixed gaze into the clear moonlight
67. since the moon had not risen yet
68. the edge of the moon appeared from behind a mass of clouds
69. a path formed by rays from the moon
70. the light of the moon resting calmly on the cypresses
71. covered with gleams of the moon, seemed like dream visions
72. moon rose large and full from behind the mountains
73. the moon shone so brightly that they put out their torches
74. dancing by the light of the moon

75. and rays of the moon, entering through an opening in the roof, filled the place with silvery light
76. the sad light of the moon
77. pale moon moving among the trees shone with uncertain light
78. gleamed from afar in the moonlight
79. moon shone with full light
80. the moon being clouded presently is missed
81. the moon was so bright that there were dark shadows cast
82. moon had been lighted and was hung in a treetop
83. white and awful the moonlight reached over
84. the slow rising of the round moon
85. moon colored by the reflected light
86. warm lie the yellow beams of moon
87. the moon, though not more than half full, threw a spirited and enticing brightness upon the fantastic figures

SS1-14 (SKYSCAPES - STARS)

1. a fine starlit sky lit the dark
2. night sky is a black dome with tiny sparks
3. under a sky full of eternal eyes
4. a flying star shot through the sky
5. a constellation in the sky
6. spangled heavens
7. sparkle the crowd of stars
8. soft white stars were shining in the wide sky
9. in the sleeping sky
10. night trailed her robe of jewels
11. a pale star gleams
12. the stars seemed dying away in the brightening sky
13. stars were shining coldly in a cloudless sky
14. a sky full of silver sheen and radiance
15. shimmering, pearl-like sparkle of an evening star
16. the whole sky was blazing with stars

17. stars seemed actually suspended from the dark vault of heaven
18. crowning itself with a diadem of his magnificent stars
19. overhead the sky was radiant with stars
20. all speckled with stars
21. that blessed star
22. the stars come out and twinkle in the sky
23. if there are stars, you can lie and try to count how many
24. scarcely ever any stars
25. as the stars began to kindle their trembling lights
26. the stars shone in upon them
27. stars blinked out
28. a bright star exactly over me
29. looks at the star in our zenith, as it hangs low upon his horizon
30. a star appeared, and another, and another
31. stars sparkled amid the yards and rigging, as if they had been tiny lamps suspended in the ropes
32. morning star is lovely over there
33. star dissolved into the day
34. morning star melts away into the light of heaven
35. among the stars
36. one or two faint stars blinking through rifts in the night
37. winter came with the stars
38. whole sky was blazing with stars
39. stars were larger and brighter than they appear through the dense atmosphere
40. crowning itself with a diadem of his magnificent stars
41. a few stars were shining
42. up toward the lustrous evening star
43. radiant star
44. the stars over us were sparkling ever so fine
45. the sky, up there, all speckled with stars
46. watched the stars that fell
47. the single stars which are sprinkled through the sky

48. stars to guide
49. what the stars decree
50. observes the stars, and notes their sliding course
51. not one star was kindled in the sky
52. stars were muffled
53. twinkling stars arise
54. stars in silent order moved around
55. morning had chased away the flying stars
56. when the stars descend, and when they rise
57. serenely shone the stars
58. when the setting stars are lost in day
59. the bright evening star began to rise
60. struck the golden stars
61. observing the courses of the stars
62. the region of the summer stars
63. the air being cleared, the stars began to appear
64. gazes on the stars
65. last star in the tail of the Little Bear is the Polestar
66. stars withdrew, marshaled by the Day-star
67. a shooting star which marks the heavens with its brightness as it falls
68. heaven with all its stars
69. sprang that yellow star from downy hours
70. the evening star quivered in the misty air
71. the soft white stars were shining in the wide sky above the river
72. how white the stars are
73. under the cold, splendid stars
74. a fixed star to steer by
75. guided by the stars
76. a beautiful star! how clear and lucid
77. a star could not be more brilliant
78. gazing on the sparkling stars
79. small stars popped and winked and hopped in vastness of blue

80. the stars are distinctly visible
81. black and empty sky where a pale star gleams
82. on high the stars seemed dying away in the brightening sky
83. the glittering star
84. millions of stars were lighted
85. saw a star begin to burn
86. soon a star arose
87. under the stars, which never seemed so bright and so near
88. a star glowed with steady luster
89. garlands of star-clusters
90. the twinkling of the stars
91. the glitter of innumerable twinkling stars
92. more brilliant than the brightest star that illumes the earth
93. countless as the stars
94. followed the movement of the stars and counted their course
95. stars lighten the blackness
96. good star shine down upon thee
97. hinder the decree of the stars
98. stronger than the light of all the stars
99. all the stars were shining with the radiance of the full moon
100. a bright star of eminence shines forth
101. in the heavens shone the stars' fair light
102. swift as the sparkle of a glancing star
103. such a scant allowance of star-light
104. the stars are glorious and beautiful in their orbs
105. stars, twinkling above the vague black hills and woods, looked down without venturing to drop their light upon them
106. stars had already richly spangled all the heavens
107. the light of the stars sufficed for all the purposes
108. the thoughtful stars were glimmering in their mild glory

SS1-15 (SKYSCAPES – DARK)

1. black as pitch
2. an oblong piece of dull gray sky
3. a steely blue patch
4. darkness gains upon the sky
5. no promise of day was in the murky sky
6. night sky is a black dome with tiny sparks
7. night sky is a black wall
8. the cold black of the night sky
9. sky grew black with the dust
10. darkness is piled upon darkness
11. a gloom as of twilight
12. the dark background of the sky
13. dark shield of the sky
14. not one star was kindled in the sky
15. darkness thickened
16. yard was so dark that he was fain to grope with his hands
17. darkness is cheap
18. upon the bleak, dark night
19. it was so dark that, looking out of bed, he could scarcely distinguish the transparent window from the opaque walls
20. endeavoring to pierce the darkness with his ferret eyes
21. darkness and the mist had vanished with it
22. move on through the lonely darkness
23. separate it from the darkness by which it was surrounded
24. very dark, too dark to be observed with any accuracy
25. the stillness and the darkness
26. only the littlest little darkness
27. with the falling of the first shadow of that darkness
28. darkness was steadily growing
29. let this darkness proceed, and spread night in the world
30. blot out the sun for good
31. let the darkness grow awhile
32. got to be pitch-dark

33. in that deep darkness and that graveyard hush
34. modified the dark, just toned it down enough to make it dismal
35. darkness was so heavy that one could not see far
36. darkness came on fast
37. almost solid darkness
38. darkness that was packed and crammed in between two tall forest walls
39. was blotted out again in the darkness
40. dimly through the darkness
41. darkness and stillness reigned again
42. dark is coming on, presently
43. dark would come to our help
44. there were no lamps in those days, and it was a dark night
45. a blot upon darkness
46. it was darker and solider than the rest of the darkness
47. too dark to see anything
48. very creepy there in the dark and lonesomeness
49. on a dark winter's day
50. through strange streets where the day was as dark as the night
51. dark, foggy days in London
52. the darkness seemed more intense than any she had ever known
53. enter from the chill darkness outside
54. just after dark one evening
55. dusk had thickened into darkness
56. been hidden from us by the darkness
57. watching the lights sink to shadows, the shadows sink to darkness
58. cast tapering dashes of darkness
59. somewhere in the darkness
60. the darkness rendered the position of a person a matter of uncertainty
61. all was wrapped in a darkness

62. eyes grew accustomed to the darkness
63. evening grew dark and night came on
64. that dark, dreary horizon
65. till the chill darkness enclosed them round
66. it grew quite dark
67. lost in the darkness
68. clothed in thick darkness
69. night shut down, dark and drizzly and cold
70. it was dark and cold and wretched
71. the wall and the window looked equally dark
72. as the twilight deepened toward darkness
73. suspended from the dark vault of heaven
74. night was coming on, the darkness began to gather
75. in the gathering darkness
76. see the moon go off watch and the darkness begin to blanket the river
77. get so dark that it looked all blue-black outside, and lovely
78. dark as sin
79. the darkness soaked her up, every last sign of her
80. it begun to darken up and look like rain
81. dark wiped it all out
82. the solid dark
83. as soon as it was fairly dark
84. on a sudden the moon, which was then at full and high in the heavens,
85. the moon grew dark, and by degrees lost her light,
86. The moon passed through various colors, and at length was totally eclipsed
87. such darkness reigned around
88. easily escape under cover of the dark
89. out of darkness dawns a light
90. out of light brings power of darkness still
91. soon covered all the face of heaven with a cloak of pitchy darkness

92. one day perceived it suddenly grow dark
93. the night seems to add its own darkness
94. only in the hours of darkness
95. be consigned to darkness
96. regions of darkness and cold
97. darkness lent her sufficient cover
98. in the darkness which suddenly seemed to have become more intense
99. in the darkness which surrounded her as with a pall
100. suffocating blankness and darkness that was rising around me
101. the vastness and profundity of the quiet and the dark
102. contagious darkness in the air
103. tide of darkness flowed on swiftly

SS1-16 (SKYSCAPES – LOCATION)

1. the background of sky
2. in mid-sky
3. beneath a violet sky
4. cutting against the sky
5. sky and boundless atmosphere
6. a nether sky
7. having the sky for a top
8. it cut a dark polygonal notch out of the sky
9. spot of outer sky
10. the blue sky bends over all
11. in an open patch of sky
12. a streak of morning in the eastern sky
13. particular portion of the sky
14. the background of the crimson sky
15. earth and sky seem whirling round together
16. a remote part of the pale night sky
17. a circular rift of clear sky
18. sea and sky- merged together in one great, silent mystery

19. to where the sky stoops
20. the point of astonishment is the meeting of the sky and the earth
21. with nothing but the sky above
22. across the face of the sky
23. unknown regions of the sky
24. the sky seemed to settle down upon the earth
25. far blue arch
26. dwellings of the sky
27. it melted into the distant sky
28. the bowl of the sky
29. the floor of the sky
30. the sky, ever so blue, seemed in hand-reach
31. earth and sky seemed blended into one
32. at the dip of the sky
33. piled against the sky-line
34. on the rim of the sky
35. the opposite side of the sky
36. under a great, high-sprung sky
37. sheet of sky
38. vandyked against the sky
39. softly outlined against the sky
40. tumbling down the sky
41. a pale place in the sky
42. low down in the sky
43. from another quarter of the sky

SS1-17 (SKYSCAPES – OTHER)

1. in a melon-frame atmosphere
2. her mood was such that the humid sky harmonized with it
3. shadowy phantom figures against the sky
4. the brightness of the sky compensating for the darkness of the earth
5. the vast and sheeted sky

6.   magnificent temple of the sky
7.   earth and sky seem whirling round together
8.   a particular light in the sky
9.   a lurid light in the sky
10.   quiet as the sky
11.   the sky was a day-dream to look at
12.   the embracing sky
13.   eternal dances of the sky
14.   the solemn sky
15.   the low sky thinned a trifle
16.   it melted into the distant sky
17.   the sky is weirdly lit
18.   the sky is like an envelope
19.   the sky was a blue-domed iceberg
20.   no radiance in the far sky
21.   covers but not hides the sky
22.   lovely phantom fabric in the sky
23.   the kingdom of the sky
24.   that lick the sky
25.   sky shrank upward

SS1-18 (SKYSCAPES – RAINBOW)

1.   like a rainbow in a murky sky
2.   liquid light thrown so prodigally over the sky
3.   the rainbow set its arch in the sky
4.   stain of the rainbow fading out of the sky
5.   instantly a beautiful rainbow was formed by the spray,
      and hung in mid-air suspended over the
6.   ring-streaked-and-striped, all sorts of colors, as splendid
      as a rainbow
7.   formed a radiant rainbow
8.   has as many shades as a rainbow and every shade is the
      prettiest while it lasts
9.   measured by the arc of the rainbow

10. little young rainbows that haven't grown big yet
11. the rainbow, its hues are as various as the hues of that arch
12. watch the stain of the rainbow fading out of the sky
13. a wholly pure phenomenon like the rainbow
14. beneath a rainbow bending bright
15. we call the rainbow a mere appearance of phenomenon in a sunny shower
16. could only span it with its rainbow
17. which there hung a magnificent rainbow, like that narrow and tottering bridge
18. the rainbow giving light in the bright clouds
19. rainbow, based on ocean, span the sky
20. overhead a rainbow, bursting through the scattering clouds, shone, spanning the dark sea, resting its bright base on the quivering blue
21. quite a celestial kaleidoscope
22. so this rainbow looked like hope
23. come and go as rainbows
24. rainbow mirrors human aims and action
25. a lovely rainbow arched its radiant colors in the sun
26. with a kind of pale, dim rainbow
27. the rainbows which the son of Saturn has set in heaven as a sign to mortal men
28. downward sweep of a rainbow
29. swimming in a sea of rainbows
30. the rainbow radiance
31. prismatic colors of the rainbow
32. incandescent rainbows shone above it
33. died out in a double rainbow and a light roll of thunder
34. first rainbow that was seen in the world was a miracle
35. lovely rainbow-light falling everywhere
36. the sunlight struck them with an ever-varying rainbow bloom as they moved

37. now the sun broke forth, the rainbow appeared, and every prospect was fair
38. while a transient rainbow stole athwart the cloudy sky of despondency
39. rainbow never forms a full circle, nor any segment greater than a semicircle
40. there are never more than two rainbows at one time
41. we have only met with two instances of a moon rainbow in more than fifty years
42. the rainbow is a reflection
43. the rainbow always appears opposite the sun
44. the rainbow is distinguished by the variety of its colors
45. scattering the sunlight in a million rainbow flashes
46. make artificial rainbows
47. where the rainbow touches the earth a treasure lies buried
48. broken rainbow
49. see the shimmer of the rainbow, which unites earth to heaven
50. while the rainbow flutters about them like a many-colored ribbon
51. rainbow above in the blue heavens seemed to span the dark world
52. rainbow marks the end of storms
53. had danced blithely out to enjoy a rainbow
54. the same instant a rainbow radiance flashed along
55. the play of water formed a rainbow
56. a rainbow in brilliancy
57. heaven spreads their peace and fame upon the arch of the rainbow
58. and a rainbow, spirit of all the colors that adorned the earth and sky, spanned the whole arch with its triumphant glory
59. a fanciful treasure at the base of some rainbow, retreating over hill and water-fall, to lure pursuit and disappoint hope

60.   rainbow, resting its further end just where, in autumn, I had marked the spot
61.   it was in this lovely spot that the rainbow at last materialized
62.   on motley rainbow-arches
63.   like the rainbows of the ocean, that could rival in color the most beautiful tropical birds
64.   a stray beam from a rainbow
65.   its ever radiant rainbow
66.   a lake of rainbow light
67.   a rainbow above the eastern woods promised a fair evening
68.   segment of the rainbow which I have clutched
69.   rainbows, crimson and azure and emerald, were broken in star-showers
70.   by the glory of a rainbow
71.   the rainbows of the west were gone; emerald and topaz, amethyst and ruby, had faded into silver-gray
72.   flashing fresh rainbows at every shifting of the lights
73.   ringed with gay rainbows
74.   where the rainbow touches the ground, always a field beyond you
75.   formed a broken rainbow of all hues quivering in the ascending streams of azure mist, until they seemed to melt and mingle with the very heavens
76.   rainbow hung upon it for a moment
77.   a wrecked rainbow, melted away in radiant streams

SS1-19 (SKYSCAPES – FOG)

1.   tides of mist
2.   eerie mist hovering
3.   dingy mist
4.   under a thin cloak of fog

5.   vague green mists
6.   tongue of fog
7.   under an overcast sky
8.   the wisps of mist that had drifted upriver from the estuary were soon spirited away by the sun
9.   the sky was entirely overcast
10.   grey heavy sky
11.   the low, dirty sky
12.   the pale white spot of a sun
13.   the sky was a pit of bale and dread
14.   the sky was a tatter of gray
15.   a sudden dullness had dropped from the sky
16.   the sky seemed a grey mantle
17.   bathed in ghostly day
18.   misty blue sky
19.   with no visible rays
20.   a sky of ashen hue
21.   a sky the sun did not illuminate
22.   the quiet sky asserted its presence overhead as a dim grey sheet of blank monotony
23.   Presently the sky became overcast
24.   small curling mists lay
25.   airy shreds and ribbons of vapor floated about
26.   fog came pouring in, and was so dense that the houses opposite were mere phantoms
27.   the dingy cloud come drooping down, obscuring everything
28.   fog and darkness thickened so
29.   a dense and billowy fog
30.   the yellow fog hung so thick
31.   and over everything the pall of drizzle and fog
32.   there began to hang a white ribbon of fog
33.   the impenetrable solidity of the fog
34.   answered from out the far distances of the fog
35.   a smoky fog of clouds covered the whole region densely

36. the fog shut down on us once more
37. smothered in the fog again
38. monstrously magnified by the fog
39. see the fog closing down
40. shot out into the solid white fog
41. dismal and lonesome out in a fog
42. river was streaked with fog
43. a fog is always favorable to a hunted enemy
44. always the most frightful fog
45. screened by a fog
46. a thick gray fog brooded over the land
47. a thick fog hid the land from our sight
48. fog began to rise, and seemed to be lifted up from the water like a curtain
49. light fog ascended to the ceiling
50. a semi-transparent fog
51. the shreds of fog here and there raggedly furring her
52. the dim, fog-draped streets
53. fog still hung about and screened us with its friendly shade
54. a heap of fog and duskiness
55. on the lake where fog trails and mist creeps
56. a pearl fog
57. were only fog, dew and vapor
58. bleak unkindly fog
59. thick fog rolled down
60. fog was creeping over the desolate flat
61. smell the fog that hung about the place
62. a drizzling rain and a dark-brown fog
63. gathering fog towards the twinkling lights of the town
64. frequent fog-banks gave them cause to doubt
65. masses of sea-fog came drifting inland- white, wet clouds, which swept by in ghostly fashion, so dank and damp and cold

66. a mass of dank mist, which seemed to close on all things like a gray pall
67. the blanket of fog
68. still fog, which the sunrise cannot pierce
69. fog, which had evidently grown thicker and poured into the room
70. soon a dense fog enveloped the ship
71. soon the fog begin to melt away
72. fog fell on us
73. the fog had a fruity taste of youth
74. when fog conceals
75. suddenly a gross fog over-spread with his dull vapor
76. fair morning clad in misty fog
77. fog, which for a moment hung in the sunny air
78. fog had by this time saturated the trees
79. getting indistinct in the fog and gloom
80. fog, which hung between them like blown flour
81. sheltered from the damp fog
82. we were compassed round by a very thick fog
83. dust-filled air muffled sound more completely than fog does
84. a kind of illuminated fog
85. there was a white fog, very warm and clammy, and more blinding than the night
86. behind the blind whiteness of the fog
87. the fog from off the water
88. the huge lake of fog which lay over
89. there hung a dense, white fog
90. the fog-wreaths came crawling round both corners of the house and rolled slowly into one dense bank
91. through the fog, as through a curtain, there stepped the man
92. from the shadows of the fog
93. broke upon us out of the wall of fog
94. fog-bank lay like white wool against the window

95. struggled through the fog
96. with a certain thickness of fog
97. the marsh-gendered fog conceal it not
98. when a fog disperses gradually
99. dizzy altitudes among fog-wreathed peaks
100. darkened by a drizzling yellow fog
101. blended with the frozen fog
102. make our way through this atmospheric fog
103. penetrate through the distant fog
104. the veil which concealed the mysterious distance
105. a thicker fog upon the still and heavy air
106. fog had by this time become more translucent
107. a clammy fog blew through the town
108. moved through the white fog which enveloped
109. fog of the previous day or two had traveled up here by now
110. chilly fog from the meadows
111. the fog dew dripping off the brim of his cap

SS1-20 (SKYSCAPES – LIGHTS)

1.   reddening the distant sky
2.   in the abyss of brightness
3.   the sky had a tallow gleam
4.   the sky is weirdly lit
5.   a reddish light in the sky
6.   like the glow of an immense forge
7.   all the eastern sky began to silver and shine
8.   sky was lurid with light cast up from
9.   the northern lights threw their mysterious glare far over the horizon
10. the sky, with all its variety of light
11. gentle light shed a fairylike gleam
12. rich greenish radiance sprang into the sky
13. waving to and fro like pale green flames

14. the lights shine there at night
15. the only lights were some spots of dull red, glowing here and there
16. as the stars began to kindle their trembling lights
17. watching the lights sink to shadows
18. the spotty lights and shades from the shining moon
19. lights shone upon them from the horizon and from the sky
20. two placid lights like rayless stars
21. jeweled with twinkling lights
22. a dull blur of lights
23. remote little sparkle of lights glinting high aloft among the stars
24. the spectacle of the dying lights of day
25. flashing forth sinister lights
26. among the living lights of heaven
27. a strange flickering light, which flashes up over the northern skies
28. scattered lights in the starry firmament
29. the northern lights threw their mysterious glare far over the horizon
30. the heavenly firmament decked with lights
31. the moon's mystic shimmer was casting a million lights across the distant,
32. restless water
33. the water gleamed with the million lights of the sun
34. the silver dance of the mystic northern lights
35. the Northern Lights are the glare of the Arctic ice and snow
36. freakish flights of strange oily lights
37. the night is splendid in the gleam of the Northern Lights
38. the stars and lights of heaven
39. lights in the firmament of the heaven
40. the glare from the lights above beat down upon
41. a great number of lights which looked exactly like stars in motion

42. bright with galaxies of immutable lights
43. the magical lights of the horizon
44. the lights were as those of a camp in heaven
45. among the lights of heaven
46. the northern lights shot forth red and blue flames, like continuous fireworks
47. a random shower of amber lights
48. a narrow galaxy of lights
49. a muster of northern lights reared their dim lances
50. the sun made vivid lights and shades on
51. a greenish wave of the Northern Lights would roll across the hollow of the high heavens
52. lights twinkled here and there in the darkness
53. the lights of heaven are surrounded by a halo
54. flashed out a medley of sparkling lights

SS1-21 (SKYSCAPES – HORIZON)

1. a great distance below the horizon
2. stretching away in billowy perspective to the horizon
3. a moving black mass under the horizon
4. it was reposing on the horizon with a calm luster of benignity
5. it was visible to a width of half the horizon
6. the horizon met the eye with the effect of a vast concave
7. across the horizon, piercing the firmamental luster like a sting
8. the horizon's warm light flooded her face
9. the sun was within ten degrees of the horizon
10. the changeless horizon of the sea
11. the horizon which lay like a line ruled from hillside to hillside
12. lights shone from the horizon and from the sky
13. like a floating and transparent veil cast onto the horizon
14. reflecting the horizon it seemed like a patch of blood

15. fantastic and striking horizon
16. went into ecstasies over the far-stretching horizon
17. see the round sun once more before he disappears beneath the horizon
18. its head pointed straight towards the horizon
19. stretched along the western horizon
20. crescented on the rim of the horizon
21. overreaching the wide horizon
22. pursuing the horizon
23. the vacant horizon
24. and the horizon became dim to me
25. horizon shows black against the sky, broken only by the fantastic silhouette
26. to the star-drift on the horizon rim
27. stormy quarters of the horizon
28. the horizon was restored to serenity and silence
29. glide my eye over the horizon of the lake
30. limit his horizon to the passing hour
31. on the blue horizon
32. within the widest horizon
33. transcendent region beyond my horizon
34. universal and true horizon
35. extending to the horizon
36. is golden in the horizon
37. except for one little threatening cloud on the horizon
38. sunk beneath the horizon
39. on the horizon, with a strip of silvery light from the unseen sun
40. along the northern horizon
41. as the sun drew near the horizon
42. clouds broke a little near the horizon in that quarter of the heavens
43. horizon was covered with a singular copper-colored cloud
44. low line of the horizon

45. the sun is high over the distant horizon, which seems jagged, with
46. trees or hills
47. it is so far off that big things and little are mixed
48. horizon is lost in a gray mist; all is vastness
49. clouds are still aglow with the rays streaming above the horizon
50. that beautiful sun began to climb the horizon
51. stretching in a long line to the horizon
52. horizon widened out in endless waves of confusion
53. far beyond the curvature of the horizon
54. sun sinks to rest in the horizon
55. there is rejoicing in the horizon
56. dwell in the uttermost limits of the horizon
57. cometh forth from the horizon
58. like the horizon, is always equally remote in all directions
59. much as the horizon recedes before a moving sea ship
60. parallel to the horizon
61. the darkness receding on the limits of the horizon
62. bar of cloud that sleeps on the horizon
63. the ideas which have emerged on their mental horizon
64. learned of the horizon the art of perpetual retreating and reference
65. magical lights of the horizon
66. the horizon was a mysterious sheet of fathomless shade
67. preternatural inversion of light and shade
68. half of the horizon from which the storm threatened
69. well defined against the sunny portion of the horizon
70. the sun was upon the verge of the horizon
71. ocean appeared at a distance and formed the utmost boundary of the
72. horizon
73. the horizon had cut off his light
74. follow the stars from the one horizon to the other
75. dawning in the horizon

76. horizon is fiercely naked- not the thinnest cover of a soft cloud, not the vaguest hint of a distant cool shower
77. red sun touched the horizon and spread out like a jellyfish
78. the thrust of light still flowed up from the western horizon
79. stars flowed down in a slow cascade over the western horizon
80. over the abyss of the horizon
81. horizon was almost equally gloomy, with scarcely one light spot
82. sets the bounds between the enlightened and dark parts of things
83. horizon all golden from the sunken sun
84. hung in the pearly horizon
85. the horizon of remote antiquity
86. the horizon bounded by a propitious sky, azure, marbled with pearly white
87. horizon, now perfectly calm, pure, and free from all haze
88. clouds are falling lower and lower upon the sea, as if to crush it

SS1-22 (SKYSCAPES – MIST)

1. tides of mist
2. eerie mist hovering
3. dingy mist
4. vague green mists
5. under an overcast sky
6. the wisps of mist that had drifted upriver from the estuary were soon spirited away by the sun
7. the sky was entirely overcast
8. grey heavy sky
9. the low, dirty sky
10. the pale white spot of a sun
11. the sky was a pit of bale and dread
12. the sky was a tatter of gray

13. a sudden dullness had dropped from the sky
14. the sky seemed a grey mantle
15. bathed in ghostly day
16. misty blue sky
17. with no visible rays
18. a sky of ashen hue
19. a sky the sun did not illuminate
20. the quiet sky asserted its presence overhead as a dim grey sheet of blank monotony
21. presently the sky became overcast
22. small curling mists lay
23. airy shreds and ribbons of vapor floated about
24. the moon's insufficient light would soon die out in the mist on the horizon
25. a red mist, in the midst of the phosphorescent scintillations of the ocean
26. the coast was visible through the broken mist
27. the sun's disc, enlarged by the mist, seemed an enormous ring of gold
28. the light appeared larger through the mist
29. the mist narrowed the horizon around her
30. as red as the sun's disk when it sets in the mist
31. a mist of colour
32. the wind swept a mist of tiny crystals through the air
33. the clouds were a misty shadow
34. a light bluish mist-like a floating and transparent veil cast onto the horizon
35. a kind of transparent mist, like a spider's web
36. the sun, half curtained in fleecy mist
37. an exceedingly great mist of darkness
38. silver with clinging mist
39. creeping blue mist
40. the impalpable mist
41. a thick milky mist hung over
42. a drizzly mist

43. the mist resembles the rain
44. everything was enveloped in a thick mist
45. the horizon is lost in a grey mist
46. half shrouded in the mist
47. the inrushing mist swept with it the surface of the sea
48. a mass of dank mist seemed to close on all things like a grey pall
49. a thin streak of white mist
50. a thin mist began to creep up from the river
51. wreaths of mist
52. a mist of changing hue
53. smooth semilucent mist
54. the preternatural mist
55. whiff of mist
56. there were heaps of hoary mist
57. seemed to be seething in a mist of heat
58. a drift of mist on the moon
59. a foggy mist overcast the day
60. a mist was dimly perceived to be escaping into the night air
61. the sun went down in an ochreous mist
62. scrolls of mist rolling over
63. boughs were beaded with the mist
64. mist hung like a magnificent silvery veil
65. mist made the night more dark
66. the mist was a filmy haze
67. covered and hidden in the mist
68. morning's fragrant mist
69. the clouds changed into a mist
70. thick clouds of mist
71. rosy light shone through the silver mist
72. in sea-green mist, the morning steals
73. swathed in a shadowy mist
74. indistinct in a pearly mist
75. a cold silvery mist had veiled

76. stars were shining beyond the mist
77. amid a gathering mist, gilded by the last sunbeams
78. the mist was like a gauzy and radiant fabric
79. blurred by a creeping mist
80. whole valley was bathed in golden mist
81. at dawn a fruitful mist is spread over the earth
82. through the shining mist of morning
83. wrapped deep in mist
84. the nightly moonshine interwove itself with the morning mist
85. a death-white mist swept over
86. the south wind spread a curtain of mist over
87. a light, airy veil of mist
88. a creamy mist so rich, so soft, so enchantingly vague and dreamy
89. a golden mist of sunset
90. through a tinted mist
91. shreds out in a fringe of mist
92. a veil of shimmering mist
93. glimmering through a tinted, exquisite mist
94. a pale bank of mist
95. mist magnified the moon
96. lost by degrees in the mist
97. the thinning mist dissolved altogether
98. the blue-white mist over the
99. all the mist about him seemed to be full of rolling, wavy shadows
100. with a wisp of mist
101. a little mist of spray
102. the morning mist swept off in a whorl of silver
103. a long, lazy, round-shouldered bank of mist, as yet untouched by the morning sun
104. curious gauzy mist
105. the landscape was wreathed in billows of morning mist
106. diaphanous wreaths of mist

107. a thin and ghastly mist
108. a thin and dull mist gathered over
109. a dense bed of mist
110. the mist, gloomily empurpled, magnified the star
111. a wintry mist mingled with a sepulchral vapour
112. the mist from without entered and spread about like a whitish wadding picked apart by invisible fingers

SS1-23 (SKYSCAPES - SUNRISE)

1. sun clears the horizon
2. fires of sunrise
3. the sun's disc bisected the horizon
4. the rising sun only began to burn away the morning mist
5. bleak early moments of sunrise
6. wan yellow light of dawn
7. true blaze of sunrise arose above the last vestiges of night
8. umber light painted across the sky
9. it was just beginning to grow light
10. the pale light of dawn
11. the morning dawned frosty and bright
12. pale glow of the sky
13. it was mere wan lightness first
14. rosy sky spread over the eastern land
15. lustrous yellows in the east
16. a streak of morning in the eastern sky
17. the pale light in the sky where the day was coming
18. no promise of day was in the murky sky
19. red lighting of the sky
20. the eastern sky began to quicken
21. the magical lights of the horizon
22. morning rends the vaulted sky
23. cleft the night with a wavy golden edge
24. the stars seemed dying away in the brightening sky
25. drowsing earth between the day and night

26. all the eastern sky began to silver and shine
27. the gray dawn streaked the sky
28. that gloomy moment usually precedes the dawn
29. the full triumph of light over darkness
30. shone like a great rose window at the end of a cathedral aisle
31. the morning dawned pearly and lustrous
32. holy hush of silvery sky
33. a sky that was pale golden and ethereal
34. gloried over with trails of saffron and rosy cloud
35. the eastern sky was all silvery and cloudless
36. the east reddens up
37. the sun came climbing up over the mountains at a very early hour during these summer months
38. a sunrise that feeds and refreshes the soul
39. the peculiarity of sunrise is to make us laugh at all our terrors of the night
40. they saw above their heads a gleam of sunrise
41. the sunrise was the kind that foretells a calm day
42. warm winds blow from the place of sunrise
43. it was now clear sunrise
44. a sunrise that crimsoned sky and sea
45. the day was cloudy and unsettled at sunrise
46. after sunrise, the mist became more transparent
47. at sunrise there was very little wind
48. a light breeze sprang up at sunrise from the east
49. the morning was grey, wild, and melancholy
50. at sunrise, the sky was still temperate and clear
51. towards sunrise there's a keen wind blowing from off the river
52. sunrise with its flaring spokes of light
53. glittering arrows of morning
54. a wide sunrise in the dawn
55. the sun rose above the horizon
56. a beautiful summer sunrise

57. sunrise threw a golden beam
58. the yellow sunrise broadened behind the hills
59. the silvery luster preceding a hot day trembled across the sleeping fields
60. it was a hazy sunrise
61. in the midst of a golden sunrise
62. a cheery sunrise kindled a golden sparkle
63. all the pines on the mountain were fired by sunrise
64. the sun sprang out of bed and the world was golden in an instant
65. a red, windy sunrise
66. the clouds cleared away at sunrise
67. sunrise transformed the mountain from a corpse-like gray to a rosy enchantment
68. sunrise sets the whole world to a new tune
69. as the sun rose, the outline of the mountain gradually faded away in the glare of the eastern sky
70. sunrise appeared to hang fire
71. the glow of the sunrise
72. the banners of the sunrise were shaken triumphantly across the pearly skies
73. the very earliest beams of sunrise saluted the

WS
(WATERSCAPES)

WS2-1 (WATERSCAPES - WATERFALLS)

1. gleaming waterfalls
2. curtain of falling water
3. under mists of spray
4. from which leaped a waterfall
5. the hoarse waterfall replied with its echoes
6. dim haze which hung over the Waterfall
7. the high waterfall of some mighty river

8.   upon a gentle waterfall
9.   the white line that the waterfall makes
10. the appearance of a trickling waterfall
11. steps leading to the waterfall
12. a rich golden and crimson waterfall
13. some mighty waterfall
14. the soft murmur of the waterfall
15. making the spray sparkle with all the colors of the rainbow
16. the monstrous wall of water thundering down from above
17. atop a very high waterfall
18. a shimmering waterfall turned to burnished metal by a dying sun
19. a mighty waterfall that filled the narrow gorge from side to side
20. overhanging waterfall
21. a romantic waterfall
22. a second fall, seemed to seek the abyss
23. the stream was received in a large natural basin
24. where the waterfall comes over the cliff
25. by the side of this waterfall a narrow path climbs upward
26. the sough of the waterfall upon the rocks below
27. the everlasting sparkle of the waterfall
28. an inverted cascade is there- as perfect as the Niagara Falls
29. at the foot of the falls, where the water is quite still
30. rise in a seven-stepped stairway of foamy and glittering cascades
31. the crystal streams descend in murmuring falls
32. crystal stream falls over the ledges of a high precipice
33. every drop as it falls assuming the prismatic colors of the rainbow
34. running over the precipice it was dispersed in spray before
35. falling like rain upon projecting ledges

36.   which leaped a mountain stream in a fall of sixty feet
37.   the hoarse waterfall replied with its echoes
38.   some mighty waterfall which shall cast us into the abyss
39.   the fall of an immensely distant waterfall
40.   the soft murmur of the waterfall
41.   wind began in to rush out from behind the waterfall, which seemed determined to sweep us from the bridge, and scatter us on the rocks and among the torrents below
42.   the dull but increasing roar of the waterfall
43.   a mighty waterfall that filled the narrow gorge from side to side
44.   in front of a romantic waterfall
45.   where the waterfall comes over the cliff
46.   the sough of the waterfall upon the rocks below
47.   eyes fixed on the everlasting sparkle of the waterfall
48.   the dying voice of the waterfall
49.   a waterfall leaped from under a crag
50.   a dim haze hung over the waterfall
51.   the high waterfall of some mighty river
52.   the white line that the waterfall makes
53.   a rich golden and crimson waterfall
54.   a cascade appeared through the trees
55.   the spray sparkled with all the colors of the rainbow
56.   the monstrous wall of water thundering down from above
57.   a shimmering waterfall turned to burnished metal by a dying sun
58.   overhanging waterfall
59.   the waterfall, formed by this little stream
60.   where the bubbles of the fall subsided, the basin exquisitely clear
61.   the everlasting sparkle of the waterfall

WS2-2 (WATERSCAPES - STREAMS)

1.   thread of a stream

2. secluded shady nook by this purling stream
3. above thereby was the head of the stream
4. a great stream of clear water burst forth by miracle in a desert place
5. along the grassy bank of a rushing stream of clear water
6. a clear stream trickles from above
7. in the spray of a stream of clear water that sprang from a rock wall
8. a silvery stream winding among the meadows
9. place where a stream had changed its course and plunged down a mountain
10. a shady nook where a cool stream flowed
11. along the reedy stream
12. a stream silently flowing, so clear, that you might count the pebbles on the bottom
13. the bank of a stream that sloped gradually down to the water's edge
14. a mass of rock, from which a trickling stream flows
15. the stream of a river rendered turbid by rains
16. calm water at the mouth of a gentle stream
17. like a spring of water, out of a cleft in the earth
18. a pretty stream of pure water
19. on the banks of a wandering stream
20. that crosses a rushing stream
21. a vagrant stream that dallies for a time with each flower upon its bank
22. a stone on the margin of the stream
23. the low tinkling sound of an unseen stream that ran under the covert of the bushes
24. the stream broke into two branches
25. a beautiful little stream which flows down from the hills and throws itself into the river
26. the meadows by some gliding stream
27. a quiet, well-conducted little stream
28. over a rushing turbulent stream

29. the softly-gliding stream
30. by the murmuring stream
31. the stream that was traveling toward the lake
32. the moonlit stream was a python, silver, sinuous, vast
33. a stream which was very much swollen
34. smooth stream, which seemed motionless, without current or eddy
35. passed between some fields through which flowed a stream
36. a stream flowing with the volume of a river between the banks
37. the stream ran merrily over a flag spotted with bright moss
38. the gurgle of the stream was constantly in ear
39. a small lake formed by the spreading out of the stream
40. the stream rushed on stronger and stronger
41. a little stream flowing smoothly over its pebbles
42. the stream widened as they went further on
43. the dull waters of the dusky stream
44. a fine stream winding at the foot of
45. the gloomy and precarious stream
46. this small stream was a foaming torrent of the most formidable magnitude

WS2-3 (WATERSCAPES - RIVERS)

1. a deep valley which nursed a river
2. river was a twisting vein of blue
3. the foaming stream of the river
4. the majestic lake which gives birth to the impetuous river
5. by the banks of the gulfing river
6. the whelming eddies of the river
7. on the river, the water is far too wide
8. the broken bed of the river
9. at the mouth of the river

10. a small river runs and rushes into fearful chasms
11. driving the river backwards till it overflowed
12. on the banks of a broad solitary river
13. the wide deserted river
14. by the brink of the river
15. the river, descending down a little hill into a valley
16. intersected by the waving lines of river
17. the short turns of the river
18. the gloomy character of the shaded river
19. following the river to its source
20. the head-waters of the river
21. the river still rushed through its bower of trees
22. following the general direction of the river
23. the tranquil stream of this pleasant river
24. sweep the outside edge of a river clear
25. the little river, runs through a deep valley
26. a thin mist began to creep up from the river
27. a good stretch of river
28. with the cold from the river seeming to rise up
29. endless streams running down from the mountains into the river
30. the river lying like a black ribbon in kinks and curls as it wound its way
31. beside the brimming river
32. there crept out a narrow and deep river
33. the margin of the river
34. the banks of the great grey-green, greasy river
35. the river making a close and handsome curve around
36. a river, clear, brimful, and flush
37. by a river glade
38. the shallows of a river nook
39. the river runs as well above ground as below
40. the channel of a river
41. the shore of a little river
42. the river overflowing forms a quantity of marsh land

43. a rapid, impetuous river
44. a rapid ghastly river
45. near the bed of the river
46. a river flowing rapidly under its ice
47. the river would be of that deep smooth sort
48. the river races in gliding precision
49. the river slid along noiselessly as a shade
50. the river hurls itself is an immense chasm
51. broad and rapid river forces its way
52. skirted by a deep and rapid river
53. the river descends rapidly, and winds between hills
54. a meandering river
55. the stream of the river was too gentle
56. the little river fell into the bay
57. river-beds swell thunderously
58. river-windings far and wide
59. dim shore of the ink-black river
60. river has drowned its banks
61. on the slope of the desolate river
62. the ripples are rampant in the river
63. the long, sudden reaches of the river
64. the river runs swiftly among the reeds
65. following the edge of the river
66. willows lined the river
67. the low leaden line beyond was the river
68. the river was just another horizontal line
69. river was a watery lead-color
70. the low grounds by the river
71. along the course of the river
72. a little garden overlooking the river
73. the wind rushed up the river
74. the river, still dark and mysterious
75. the river is broad and solitary
76. the winding river turned and turned

1. lake lying calm in the sun
2. in a large pond
3. there was a show of bubbles in the pond
4. a shallow pond three miles in diameter
5. a pond with a stream of water trickling into it from
6. a large round pond
7. the ice pond
8. the pond in the wood
9. a pond in the meadow which came up to one side of
10. pond seemed to be almost inconveniently crowded
11. a picturesque pond
12. by the pond-waters
13. along the pond-side
14. a small pond between the poplars
15. a nice little pond
16. still as a pond, deadly still
17. near the ornamental pond
18. from the neighborhood of the pond
19. a little pond for goldfish
20. the muddy pond
21. a green slimy pond
22. a pond as deep as hell
23. like a standing pond
24. in the brown pond
25. like a summer pond
26. in this enchanted pond
27. a muddy little pond
28. a frozen pond
29. the little pond was frozen under its stiff willow bushes
30. the mill-pond had its charms
31. under the waters of a large pond
32. hidden at the bottom of the pond
33. in the depths of the pond

34. the whole pond rose with a frightful roar
35. the biggest pond in all the country
36. at one end of the pond was an earthen dam
37. the pond glittered like polished metal
38. the silver spot the moon made on the surface of the pond
39. the pond glittered
40. a pond in the garden in which a fountain played
41. in the pond where it was deepest
42. a great pond, round about which grew reeds
43. down by the mill pond
44. the bit of a pond
45. a fresh-water pond
46. a pond in dimensions
47. the bit of a pond looked like the ocean
48. the water as tranquil as that of a pond
49. on the glassy pond
50. smooth and glassy as a pond
51. the bottom of a dry pond
52. the round pond
53. in some star-lit mill-pond, with lovely water-lilies
54. the pond-lilies lie on the surface of
55. the water as level as a pond, broken only by tiny ripples
56. a small pond which was reduced to its summer shallowness
57. the pond was deep under overhanging oak trees
58. clump of weeping- willows about the duck pond
59. a swift-flowing stream widened out for a space into a decent-sized pond
60. the swirling eddies of the pond
61. a modest-sized pond in the orchard
62. the pond at the bottom of the lawn
63. a gust of wind across a pond
64. the distant pond, which lay shining between the long banks of fir-trees
65. an artificial pond, three miles square

66. little pond of water, where it's hardly deep enough to drown a man
67. in a hollow beside a marshy pond
68. the brambles by the pond
69. the pond, oblong in shape, was so long, it might have been taken for a scant river
70. was as smooth as a duck-pond
71. dimples the glassy surface of the pond
72. the stony shore of the pond

WS2-5 (WATERSCAPES - LAKES)

1. lake lying calm in the sun
2. lake lying smoother than snakeskin in the sun
3. within that lake is a rock
4. the beauty of the lake had not been exaggerated
5. the lake is alive with fish, plainly visible to the eye
6. the prettiest little curving arms of the lake
7. a majestic expanse of lake and mountain scenery
8. the crystal water of the snow-fed lake
9. a lake, in the lap of the great mountains
10. a dim and dreamlike picture of watery expanses
11. the lonely little lake
12. a shallow lake full of rushes
13. in a weedy lake
14. on the brink of a lake
15. a lake embowered in woods, which screen it from the fervid rays of the sun
16. a smooth lake that seemed another sky
17. the lake fills the crater of an extinct volcano
18. the lake spread its blue sheet
19. the transparent lake, a beautiful sheet of water, reflecting like a mirror the distant mountains
20. on the bank of a small lake
21. long lake waves breaking under the sun

22. the lake hollowed out of the earth to be a receptacle for the river's overflow
23. a lake that lay at the end of the garden
24. the lake was not very large, but it seemed an ocean
25. the bed of the water was broad
26. a spray-flung curve of shore
27. a lake of marvelous beauty, asleep at the foot of the mountain
28. the lake is the mother of the great river
29. a lake fed by black-water from the river
30. the lake, cool and clear, rippling grasses but a few feet under the surface
31. the lake of sweet waters
32. the lake, with its motionless surface
33. a small lake formed by the spreading out of the stream
34. a weird lake country, sad and silent
35. on a blue burst of lake
36. the restless surge of the lake waves
37. the shores of the dark lake
38. the profound deeps of the lake
39. arm of the lake gradually contracts its water to a very narrow space
40. an orchard on the banks of that lake
41. the horizon of the lake, bounded by banks and mountains
42. upon the edge of a remarkably blue lake
43. there was a vague sheen upon the lake's surface
44. steps descended from the garden to the lake
45. the mirror-like surface of the lake
46. the lake was of a great depth
47. the lake's coloring would shame the richest sky
48. the surface of the lake as limpid as pure air
49. a lucid lake, broad as transparent, deep, and freshly fed by a river
50. small lake, evidently fed by some springs
51. the lake had been transformed into marsh land

52. the sky and lake are blue and placid
53. the lake was as transparent as plate-glass
54. vivid flashes of lightning illuminated the lake
55. the lake reflected the scene of the busy heavens
56. an enormous lake of fathomless depth
57. the lake glittered in the evening sunlight like a sheet of molten gold
58. all one dim and vague lake
59. the shadows of the trees which fell upon the lake
60. the lake pours its waters into the sea
61. a large and extensive lake formed by the waters of the river
62. an exquisite arrangement of lake, wood, and hill
63. a clear transparent lake
64. the lake, reposing within its rim of yellow hills
65. from out the bosom of the lake
66. on the shining levels of the lake
67. the lake is not a basin
68. lake is the brightest, loveliest blue that can be imagined
69. a plain and an unshaded lake
70. magnificently pictured in the polished mirror of the lake
71. solemn, sailless, tintless lake
72. the scenery of the lake was tame and uninteresting

WS2-6 (WATERSCAPES - OCEAN)

1. a wide crescent of beach
2. the tide lapped over the road and slowly drew back, leaving a shining trail of mud
3. the everlasting stretch of ocean
4. ocean blueness deepened its color as it stretched to the foot of the crags, where it terminated in a fringe of white
5. moan of that unplummetted ocean below and afar
6. the smooth ocean rolls her silent tides
7. impetuous ocean roars

8. the powers of ocean
9. into that deep ocean by which the earth is surrounded
10. the earth sinks into the ocean
11. distant roaring of a vast ocean
12. solemn grandeur of the ocean
13. like the surges of the ocean
14. ocean- that wide and nameless sepulcher
15. the ocean beneath was clearly visible on account of its phosphorescence
16. dusky expanse of ocean
17. the billowy ocean
18. the roaring depths of ocean
19. the salty waves of the ocean
20. huge and hideous ocean
21. the deep blue of the ocean
22. the ocean of everlasting darkness
23. the broad ocean agitated by storms cannot be called sublime
24. the dark tempestuous ocean
25. the boundless ocean rising with rebellious force
26. the violet rim of the ocean
27. ocean's waters wore an inky hue
28. the ocean glittered like a lake
29. a rosy ocean, vast and bright
30. the silent ocean
31. the billowy plains of ocean
32. the surf of a wild ocean
33. the ocean, with its purple sense of solitude and void
34. the green water of the deep-sea ocean
35. the ocean rolled a lengthened wave to the shore
36. the roarings of the giant ocean
37. a wilderness of ocean
38. a boundless sheet of apparently unruffled ocean
39. the wild and wasteful ocean
40. the ocean with its moaning waves

41. the shore of deep swirling Ocean
42. the billows of a troubled ocean
43. the broad ocean was heaving its billows about
44. the surface of a storm-beaten ocean
45. the ocean had retreated rapidly from the shore and an utter darkness lay over it

WS2-7 (WATERSCAPES - CHANNEL)

1. the channel of the path
2. trickled along a channel in the midst
3. meandering along a central channel in the rocky bed of the winter current
4. narrow rafts slip along through the central channel
5. furious rapid which marred the channel
6. boats didn't always run the channel
7. just a narrow channel between
8. passed the shallow channel
9. flowing continuously in a single channel
10. river's narrow channel
11. from the greater into the smaller channel
12. a deep channel
13. a blind channel, in the bed of the creek
14. ran in a very low and hollow channel
15. formed a channel to its own brook, sometimes bordered by steep banks of earth
16. form a strait channel, something resembling the lock of a canal
17. this slender channel
18. so as to form a triangular channel
19. at the mouth of the channel which led to the sea
20. now a dry channel overgrown with leaves
21. like a tributary channel
22. a brook that had dug a channel for itself into the earth
23. portions of the channel close upon the shore

24. made the channel too boisterous to be thought of
25. the channel grew more narrow
26. channel now became a gorge
27. threaded the mazes of this channel
28. glides magically into the winding channel
29. dried river-channel
30. the channel lay clear
31. into the very channel where it ought to flow
32. channel a few atoms wide
33. filling up the channel
34. plunging into the channel of a river
35. an unobstructed channel
36. for the channel growing shallower
37. the river returned to its channel
38. sent the river flowing down a steep channel
39. the narrowness of the channel
40. dug a deep channel
41. natural channel of the river was left dry
42. channel had been bridged successfully
43. force the stream from its present channel
44. diverted into another channel
45. clearing the entrance into the channel between the island and the shore
46. the torrents tear many a new channel
47. entered the tortuous channel
48. a subterranean channel leads directly into the water
49. deep and precipitous channel
50. made a miry channel
51. to a craggy pass in the channel
52. the shallows of its own strait channel
53. struck against the rocky sides of the channel
54. a channel divided them
55. filled and overflowed its channel
56. the crookedness of the channel
57. on a maze of shoals without a channel

58. boat entered a narrow by-channel
59. channel at the back of the island
60. the channel to the stream gave grace
61. wind came in gusts sweeping in from the Channel
62. made a channel in the water so that she was able to pass through on dry ground
63. made a channel and stopped the flow of the water
64. the fairy pavilion seen floating upon the Channel
65. the low waters in their channel glide
66. islet and the coast were separated by a channel
67. the sand forming the bed of the channel
68. the channel lay between high banks
69. place where the channel left a ford passable at low tide
70. the channel was easily traversed
71. rendered the channel impassable
72. the depth of the channel hollowed out by the current
73. separated from the mainland by the channel
74. allowed her to reconnoiter the channel, and she boldly entered it
75. gliding up the channel
76. having seen their vessel engulfed in the channel
77. could emerge from the water of the channel
78. disappearing in the quick sands of the channel
79. diving to the bed of the channel
80. thy channel filled with waters freshly drawn
81. bid the weltering waves their oozy channel
82. Britain is separated by a shallow channel
83. along one consistent channel
84. a channel leading to them from the great vessel
85. ample space of the lower stomach into a narrower channel
86. a deep and rapid channel
87. recovered the lost channel
88. in the deepest part of the channel
89. in the plainest part of the channel

LS
(LANDSCAPES)

LS3-1 (LANDSCAPES - PLAINS)

1. grassy plains
2. dew-drenched grass glittering
3. a vast meadow stretched away to the horizon
4. the sharp green line of the western horizon
5. the top of the hill was a broad flat area of mown grass
6. on the flowery plains
7. joy of the fair plains
8. the plains, with its ripened harvests
9. wide naked plains
10. on the barren plains
11. over the grassy plains
12. plains adorned with various flowers
13. a watery dessert covers all the plains
14. the wide-stretching plains
15. water rarely appears in the plains
16. the burning sand-plains of Sahara
17. over the plains of the land's swelling bosom
18. the torrid, scented plains
19. the plains are high-lying and naked
20. the plains are covered with grass the color of a green olive
21. the wide-spreading plains
22. the plains all around were full of running streams
23. fertile and abundant plains
24. the sandy plains
25. over swelling grassy plains
26. the sparkling ice plains
27. the snow-covered plains
28. the harvests lay rich on the plains
29. the plains, soggy with water
30. level as the great harvest plains

31. enormous plains, which in winter are white with snow
32. the plains, in summer, are gray with the saline alkali dust
33. the cultivated plains
34. beautiful green plains, dotted over with clumps of towering palms
35. the plains are renowned for their beauty and extent
36. the low gravelly plains
37. into the plains rush the hills
38. a broad expanse of plains
39. a thick autumnal mist floated in waves of vapor over the plains
40. the famine-stricken plains
41. over great plains where the buffaloes live
42. upon the open plains
43. immense plains covered with rich verdure
44. a vast distance through the plains
45. the winter covers these plains in banks of snow
46. wide and treeless plains

LS3-2 (LANDSCAPES - HILLS)

1. hills formed a dark background
2. gentle wooded slopes
3. above them rose a wooded hill
4. the top of the hill was a broad flat area of mown grass
5. the white sand hills gleamed softly
6. the sand hills
7. the line of many-colored hills
8. a ridge up in the hills
9. the sand hills every day went through magical changes of color
10. the sand hills looked dim and sleepy
11. low chalky hills, intensely white, and spotted evenly with sage
12. the spotted white hills

13. the hills rose high, enclosing the town in a half-moon curve
14. sprinkled in the folds of the hills
15. a deep green valley, with distinct hills on either side
16. the farthest horizon of hills
17. great patches of the granite hills
18. surrounded by rocky, snow-clad hills
19. the summit of low hills
20. a hollow cup of hills
21. long lines of hills
22. hills of sandstone
23. the confused hills that lay before the great mountains
24. a country of little hills and hollows and rising grounds
25. low wide risings not to be called hills
26. the swelling hills of a great woodland
27. a maze of little hills
28. being rather great hills than mountains
29. the desolate hills
30. towering hills bounded the valley upon every side
31. these parched and dreary hills
32. the land rose into undulating hills
33. white peaks of the distant hills
34. an amphitheatre of hills
35. a chain of high hills
36. low hills, without trees, and almost without brush
37. the hills seem burnished with gold
38. red cindery hills
39. steep hills of granite
40. the distant wooded hills
41. abruptly conical hills
42. a low range of hills
43. the hills are of a remarkable form
44. flat gravel-capped hills
45. the hills are formed of white granular quartz rock
46. the low rounded forms of the neighboring hills

47.　irregular chains of hills

LS3-3 (LANDSCAPES MOUNTAINOUS)

1.　steep, stony climb
2.　spine of a ridge among fallen rock slabs
3.　small wooded mountain summit
4.　above the crest-line
5.　a narrow range of small mountains
6.　crest-line formed a sharp divide
7.　a confusion of random boulders
8.　from the summit of the mountain
9.　on the summit of the mountain there were several small heaps of stones
10.　the mountain began to show its true form
11.　the mountain is steep, extremely rugged, and broken
12.　a lofty and bold mountain
13.　the mountain is composed of white quartz rock
14.　blue mountain ranges in the northwest
15.　a mountain outline varies with every step, and it has an infinite number of profiles, though absolutely but one form
16.　a mountain covered with prickly points
17.　mountain-tops are bright
18.　the mountain rose above the path with almost equal inaccessibility
19.　roar of the mountain cataracts
20.　mountain ridges and passes retained their ordinary appearance of silence and solitude
21.　give them the metal our mountain affords
22.　gray March skies are curdling hard and high above the black mountain peaks
23.　mountain peaks which glowed rich orange in the last lingering sun-rays

24. bank upon bank of mountain, bathed in the yellow moonlight
25. forest of palms at the foot of a mountain eight thousand feet high
26. the mountain wall, covering the whole in deepest shade
27. the vapors had lifted from the mountain tops and were descending the long slopes
28. inaccessible cliff which formed the upper shoulder of a mighty mountain
29. shadow of the mountain
30. enable their panting lungs to endure that keen mountain air
31. mountains steep wooded slopes
32. most impressive mountain mass that the globe can show
33. the opposing mountain that towered above the trees
34. lofty mountain barrier
35. upon a barren mountain
36. grandest mountain prospect that the eye can range over
37. the impressive presence of the old mountain
38. majestic expanse of lake and mountain scenery
39. long worm of black smoke crawling lazily up the steep mountain
40. the high and woody mountain
41. a billowy chaos of massy mountain domes and peaks draped in imperishable snow
42. magnificent mountain lifts its snow-wreathed precipices into the deep blue sky
43. mountain breathed his own peace upon their hurt minds and sore hearts, and healed them
44. toiled up a steep shoulder of the mountain, clinging like flies to its rugged face
45. road was tunneled through a shoulder of the mountain

LS3-4 (LANDSCAPES - VALLEYS)

1. grassy canyons shaded by
2. shallow, dusty rise
3. a twilit canyon
4. rugged rock walls
5. a shelf of land
6. in a valley by a winding river
7. a deep valley full of stones
8. to the furthest confines of that valley
9. the northern extremity of the valley
10. the brink of a valley
11. a valley that was bounded outwardly by the sea
12. the bed of the valley
13. the innermost recesses of the lovely valley
14. the vast dim expanse of the valley
15. a fertile valley perfused by a river
16. a remote place in the valley
17. looking sheer down into the broad valley
18. the broad level green valley
19. a beautiful green valley dotted with chalets
20. across the narrow head of the valley
21. on an inconspicuous ridge in the valley
22. exquisitely green and beautiful little valley
23. the borders of the valley were wooded
24. a valley thick enclosed with cypresses and pines
25. a spacious valley, with trees gently waving to the wind
26. the mist that had risen from the valley
27. a long green little valley
28. through a narrow pass into a tiny, circular valley
29. the valley was cinched by the stark and cadaverous snows
30. deep in the trench of the valley
31. the long and broad valley through which the bright river flowed in sweeping
32. curves
33. the yawning blackness of the valley
34. a valley opening towards the sea

35. the great flat valley, green and beautiful
36. embosomed amongst a family of lofty mountains, there was a valley
37. the valley lay far below bathed in the morning sun
38. the whole valley was bathed in golden mist
39. the sultry heats and intoxicating perfumes of the valley
40. a lake stood in the center of a spacious valley
41. a broad and verdant valley, watered by a noble stream
42. a valley dense with scrub oak and fir
43. a dismal and desolate valley
44. a level, narrow valley
45. a valley, dark with wood
46. the valley ran down to a little river
47. the valley opened out into a great plain dotted over with rocks and cut up by ravines

LS3-5 (LANDSCAPES - WOODED)

1. soft green pine forests
2. in a comfortable shady grove
3. forest niche
4. trees stand silent
5. thick cloak of trees
6. band of living green
7. the trees looped and netted with shadow
8. a choice piece of parkland
9. gentle wooded slopes
10. enormous interlocked forest
11. a few pathetic trees scattered here and there
12. the wind-tossed crowns of great trees
13. under the arches of the leaves
14. tree-covered mound
15. above them rose a wooded hill

LS3-6 (LANDSCAPES - GARDENS)

1.   a trellised canopy of vines
2.   trimmed and manicured, with mown grass
3.   in a beautiful flower garden
4.   a wonderful and lovely garden
5.   this neglected garden
6.   this little garden was full of sweet flowers, half hidden by the weeds
7.   a path all round the garden
8.   old-fashioned, fragrant flowers in her garden
9.   the frost-bitten garden
10. a pleasant old garden
11. the quaint old garden had sheltered many pairs of lovers
12. an extensive garden
13. a small cleared garden, bounded with cactus hedges
14. the garden was a good deal longer than it was broad
15. little hanging garden
16. the far end of the garden
17. a garden surrounded with walls
18. a garden of enchantment
19. the hedge of his garden formed an arch over
20. the summer scents of the garden
21. the rich old garden
22. in a grassy corner of the garden
23. musk rose in the flower-garden
24. enjoying the smell of the garden at night
25. one immense kitchen garden, well laid out and carefully tended
26. a large and finely cultivated garden
27. the birds were singing more heartily in the garden
28. the garden was set with flowers of the most delicious perfume
29. the garden was illuminated and the leaves twinkled in the darkness
30. the dry garden patch smelled of drying vines

31. there was a pond in the garden in which a fountain played
32. the darkest parts of the garden
33. the garden was sweet and fresh after the rain
34. the trees in the garden were pleasant and cool
35. a beautiful garden, gay with sunshine and flowers
36. a library opening into a garden
37. a garden with an alcove in it
38. the sun shone as warmly and brightly upon it as on the magnificent garden
39. flowers
40. with bits of flower garden
41. enclosed in its own neat garden
42. from the garden there came the heavy scent of lilac
43. dew-drenched garden
44. the green, flickering, sun-lashed garden
45. a long garden, sloping down to

LS3-7 (LANDSCAPES - DESERT)

1. desert was dried up
2. an immense desert of space
3. over a vast sandy desert, in which not a shrub appears to intercept the vision to the fertile hills beyond
4. tenantless cities of the desert
5. nothing but the silent desert extended before my eyes
6. leaving nothing but a lonely desert
7. as a palm-tree rises above the shrubs of the desert
8. has been passed in the solitudes of the desert
9. the desert and the garden are ever side by side
10. a desert in its vast nakedness
11. seated on the borders of a perfect desert
12. they saw nothing but an arid desert
13. the shifting sands of the desert would soon cover it
14. the tablelands of the desert
15. the desert was still as the sky

16. in the stopping-places of the desert
17. the wastes of the desert
18. the shadeless bosom of the desert
19. the scantier meadows of the desert
20. the soft south wind blew over the desert and nursed it
21. a dry and barbarous desert
22. a gloomy desert
23. a vast and deep desert
24. in the caves of the desert
25. a piece of sandy steppe, as if cut out of the desert
26. a dead and dreary desert
27. a desert in the tropics under a vertical sun
28. the dreary desert sand
29. the yellow sun reflected on the gray desert
30. a strip of desert on either side of the road
31. a dry desert without a drop of water
32. a most deserty desert
33. in the midst of a forbidding desert
34. the general desolation of a desert
35. a level desert of yellow sand, smooth as velvet
36. in the midst of that howling desert
37. for miles on every side, stretches a weary desert of sand and gravel
38. the perilous solitudes of the desert
39. the repulsive monotony of desert Syria
40. in the flat, burning desert
41. a piece of low, broken, desert land
42. a wearier-looking desert man never saw
43. the vast expanse of rolling desert

LS3-8 (LANDSCAPES - ROADWAYS)

1. the broad sweep of the avenue
2. the spiraling path
3. a well-worn track

4. the grass shoulder
5. the steep lane
6. a muddy parking lot
7. in a lonely road, where no assistance can be procured
8. down the narrow road
9. a heavy road
10. along the road which leads across
11. a miry and sloppy road
12. upon a dusty road
13. a corner of the road
14. some little distance off the high road
15. along the road over which they had so recently traveled
16. along the open road
17. in the middle of the road
18. throwing their dark
19. shadows over the roughly paved road
20. down the dreary road
21. on the left hand of the road
22. the road became darker than ever
23. the road to the wood
24. the road leading to the
25. the road had become a marsh
26. the road was alive with people
27. the stones of the high road
28. the wrinkles of the road
29. night devoured the road
30. a river that crosses the road
31. a road that descends cliffs and canyons
32. the road that led to the mountains
33. a long lonely road
34. after a bend of the road
35. round a bend in the gloomy road
36. they left the high road for the lane
37. the garden sloping to the road
38. which fronted the road

39. fifty miles of good road
40. it was not in their direct road
41. the road with some abruptness wound into the valley
42. it had ceased to be a country-road then, and regarded itself as a street
43. down a quiet, lovely road
44. down a quiet, lovely road
45. the road led through broad pasture-lands
46. a crooked, narrow road, walled in with tall hedges
47. the first cross-road on the east side
48. the road runs by the sea
49. the road was rough and hard

LS3-9 (LANDSCAPES - FIELDS)

1. a field silver and green with ripening oats
2. long lush grass of the meadow
3. a wind-tossed field of oats
4. corn waved in the field like a yellow sea
5. a pleasant green field, with three wide-spreading oaks
6. a field of red clover in full bloom
7. a steepish downy field
8. in the drowned field
9. the innumerable horrors of the cotton field
10. a thrice ploughed fallow field
11. a field of rich garden ground
12. the buckwheat lay like a weed in the field
13. the tall straight trunk of the pine pierced the vast field
14. in the fresh clover field
15. the field which borders the trench
16. in a lonely field
17. a secluded field
18. a very wide field
19. a wide field, full of dark mountains
20. in a lower and less important field

21.   the raised-field complex among the classic lowland Maya
22.   the nearer and richer field
23.   grass in the corner of a field
24.   a field of stiff weeds and thistles
25.   viewless expanses of field and forest
26.   that stony field
27.   a rich field in springtime
28.   an unoccupied field of no great size
29.   an adjoining field studded with apple trees
30.   a vast field of neutral brown
31.   a level field of green turf, flanked on one side by sloping banks
32.   a sunny field
33.   that broad and quiet field
34.   through a fallow-field
35.   through the field the grass was green and fine
36.   the glow sank quickly off the field
37.   the sunny autumn field
38.   the field itself was coarse
39.   a hidden wild field
40.   clumps of tangled flowers which thickly sprinkled the field
41.   at the edge of the wood the bluebells had flowed over into the field
42.   great mottled stretches of forest and field
43.   one vast field abloom with open-petaled flowers
44.   the size of an ordinary field
45.   the enclosure stretched a cultivated field

LS3-10 (LANDSCAPES - BANKS)

1.   a field silver and green with ripening oats
2.   had come to a bank breast-high
3.   threw a stone over the bank, aiming it as if to go onward over the cliff

4. over the bank is a little backward current
5. high enough to get a view of the natural surface of the hill over the bank
6. vanished over the bank
7. unenclosed for miles, except by a casual bank or dry wall
8. something disturbed the outline of the bank above him
9. from the edge of the slope, and over the bank
10. lean directly upon the bank
11. behind the bank
12. on that side of the bank
13. sprang over the bank
14. behind the bank
15. upon the dizzy slope
16. pigmy crag in the bank
17. into a huge bank of livid cloud with golden edges that rose to meet it
18. arrived at the bank of the river at dawn
19. drove up the bank a few hundred yards
20. grazing the right-bank dike
21. had a low bank of fresh green willows
22. the steep bank mountains appeared in the most fantastical shapes
23. along the grassy bank of a rushing stream of clear water
24. in the steep bank of the pedestal
25. a vast black cloud-bank
26. on the left bank of the glacier
27. buried him on the bank
28. up the river bank
29. under some willows that hung over the bank
30. in the shade of the bank
31. a deep dent in the bank
32. crept up the dead water under the bank
33. down on a cut bank with smoky ghosts of big trees on it
34. raft must be butting into the bank every now and then
35. bank was caved away under one corner

36. scooting along the bluff bank in the easy water
37. near the bank, to graze the shady grove
38. high on the bank
39. wading to the bank
40. stretched himself on the green bank
41. took his seat on a high bank
42. to the bank of a stream that sloped gradually down to the water's edge
43. to the opposite bank across the roaring water
44. on the bank of the river under the open heavens
45. with the unevenness and difficult ascent of the opposite bank
46. made a breach in the bank, and a part of the river was now pouring in here
47. over the edge of a steep bank, down which they rolled
48. dig a hole in the sandy bank
49. among the flowers of the bank
50. attained the opposite bank in safety
51. on the bank of a small lake
52. like pebbles on a river's bank
53. dark holes made by a twisted root or overhanging bank
54. wet meadow that stretched along the right bank of the river
55. two armies on the bank of the Rhine
56. dwell on the conquered bank
57. advancing to the bank of the Euphrates
58. in broad daylight, when the river-bank was thronged
59. standing on the bank of the pond
60. bank of a gurgling brook
61. grassy bank beside the thick fir grove
62. perceiving the bank of the river broken down, and the water let out and overflowing the road
63. rising like a bank between the seas
64. a circular bank
65. down the bank of the bayou

66. on the right bank, slightly veiled in the morning mist
67. gathering flowers from the bank
68. a bank of blue-blackness
69. on a river bank, watching a flood go by
70. shallow bank of the bayou
71. highness of the bank which had been thrown up
72. upon the inner bank of the ditch
73. prosaic flat bank
74. retired to the bank of a flowing river
75. from the overhanging bank
76. against a high gravel bank
77. a right angle in the bank which the men had made in the course of mining
78. tree that stood on the bank of a neighboring rivulet
79. cold bank is her bolster
80. on the canal bank
81. from the high bank a broad landscape opened
82. the bank of the milky way
83. against a bank of blossoms and bright leaves
84. its immediate bank was tolerably high and quite steep
85. smaller trees that fringed the bank
86. burying himself in the bushes of the bank
87. on the brow of the bank that bounded the water
88. on a sunny bank
89. exquisite cleanness where the bank dips into the water
90. the bank slopes upward from the stream in a very gentle ascent

LS3-11 (LANDSCAPES - SHORE)

1. shore, on which the waters chafed and dashed
2. upon the adjacent shore
3. down to the shore
4. along the shore

5. nearer to the shore than to the horizon
6. seemed almost close to the shore
7. the perilous adventure by the sea-shore
8. the higher elevations along the shore were flooded
9. the inferior dignitaries of the shore
10. the squire was thrown on shore
11. brilliant green sward on its opposite shore
12. the grains of sand on the shore
13. hundreds of yards out from shore
14. a-swinging up shore in the easy water
15. the closest to the shore
16. I slid out from shore
17. I closed in above the shore-light
18. pulled up shore in the easy water
19. went for shore
20. take to the shore
21. laying at shore
22. struck out for shore
23. the left-hand shore
24. the people on shore went to bed
25. to the main shore
26. through the lower Gaul by the shore of the Adriatic Sea
27. as he wandered on the shore
28. the Romans that crowded on the shore to meet him
29. roaring along the salt sea-shore
30. wild uncultivated shore
31. friendly shore
32. the rocky shore
33. up a desert shore
34. the ports and creeks of every winding shore
35. my native shore
36. on the sounding shore
37. on the bleak shore
38. draw a line along the shore
39. this unhospitable shore

40. to leave that execrable shore
41. along the crooked shore
42. that happy shore, that seems so nigh
43. the pleasing shore
44. the rocky shore extended to the sea
45. besiege the narrow shore
46. scant landings on a shore rock-strewn
47. sandy shore
48. sea without shore
49. rambling on the shore
50. a little bay on the shore
51. rowed along the shore till they arrived at the eastern end of the sea
52. sand from the shore of all-surrounding ocean
53. the resounding shore
54. foreign shore
55. the wonders of the ocean shore
56. rolled the waves towards the shore
57. coasting along the shore
58. lined the shore
59. towards their destined shore
60. sought the nearest shore, which was the coast
61. longing to touch the opposite shore
62. rustled on the shore
63. seek the meadows by the shore
64. along the docks on the farther shore
65. within sight of the shore
66. on this charming shore
67. a peaceful shore
68. having a dry shore
69. the windings of the Asiatic shore
70. whole shore rung with wailings
71. along a barren shore
72. along a harbor shore
73. sounds like surf on a faraway shore

74. over the low-lying shore
75. the varying shore
76. beside the pebbly shore
77. low and level shore stretched down to a silent sea
78. watching the lapping of the waves upon its farther shore
79. on a lake shore in marsh country
80. on this beautiful shore
81. strung down that desolate shore
82. he would have seen the matchless shore
83. under the weather shore

LS3-12 (LANDSCAPES - CANYON)

1. a pretty little canyon
2. entered the canyon beyond the summit
3. a sudden widening and levelness of the canyon
4. the next turn of the canyon brought me to its mouth
5. the side of the canyon continued to the water's edge
6. the narrow canyon
7. at the far end of a considerable stretch of canyon
8. the canyon veered sharply to the left
9. the main canyon
10. a bend in the left-hand canyon
11. the canyon had become a rocky slit
12. the canyon rose roughly at a steep angle toward what seemed a pass between two abutting peaks
13. at the top of the canyon was a sheer drop of two or three hundred feet to the bottom of a rocky chasm
14. the canyon was cave-like
15. a canyon that lay between outlying buttresses of the mountain
16. the sheer walls of a canyon
17. under the canyon wall
18. the rapids cut through, the roaring canyon
19. a sharp north wind blowing down the deep canyon

20.   into the wind-swept canyon
21.   a deep canyon-like rift stretching from the ice wall on the north across the valley as far as the eye could reach
22.   scaling the awful walls of the canyon
23.   into the depths of the canyon
24.   the canyon walls were perpendicular cliffs
25.   the canyon walls were striped with even-running strata of rock
26.   the canyon sides were like shelving
27.   there was a gentler canyon within a wilder one
28.   there was a deep groove running along the sides of the canyon
29.   in both walls of the canyon a streak of soft rock had been washed out
30.   the canyon twisted and wound like a snake
31.   the canyon had a dozen false endings near its head
32.   at the very bottom of the canyon, along the stream
33.   above the rim of the canyon, was a flat, wind-swept tableland
34.   the second turn of the canyon
35.   the head of the canyon
36.   thin streaks of light began to reach quiveringly down into the canyon
37.   following the course of the canyon
38.   into the inner canyon
39.   the park-like canyon

LS3-13 (LANDSCAPES - FOREST)

1.   the remains of widespread woods, which were once part of that great forest
2.   a grim forest
3.   dark wet forest
4.   the forest that fringed the valley
5.   the primeval forest

6. in the depths of the forest
7. through the forest aisles
8. sleepy murmurs of the forest
9. great stretches of forest
10. the wide forest stretches
11. within the secrecy of the forest
12. the pregnant silence of the forest
13. in the forest bare and old
14. the gloomy forest
15. round the forest track
16. in the dim forest
17. into far forest solitudes, primeval, odorous, and unexplored
18. in the forest shades
19. the virgin forest
20. plunged into the deep shadows of the forest
21. the forest was dark, as a matter of course
22. the outlines of the forest were so rich and fleecy that an opening could not be seen
23. this glorious setting of forest
24. wild luxuriance of a virgin American forest
25. the belt of forest which enclosed
26. the high and gloomy vaults of the forest
27. the drapery of a dense forest
28. clothed in the richest forest verdure
29. the giants of the forest
30. the deep stillness of the somber forest
31. the arches of the forest
32. the bright green foliage of the forest
33. some warm, forest-clad land
34. the thickets of the forest
35. the venerable antiquity of a forest
36. in wild forest nook
37. revelry the oaks of the forest
38. the dark intricacy of the surrounding forest

39.	in a vast gloom of forest
40.	the silent forest was holding its breath
41.	the bleak forest
42.	long, dim stretch of forest
43.	the mighty forest-glades
44.	a wild dark forest
45.	far edge of the frowning forest
46.	had the appearance of a primeval forest
47.	a forest of tall eastern trees
48.	the forest stood up spectrally in the moonlight
49.	an impenetrable forest
50.	the face of the forest was gloomy
51.	the long shadows of the forest had slipped down hill
52.	the gloomy border of the forest
53.	music of the forest, filled the air with delicious melody
54.	the pathless forest
55.	in a dreary forest
56.	in the thickest part of the forest, grew the most beautiful blackberries
57.	endless ranks of lofty forest trees
58.	a forest of graceful needles, shimmering in the amber sunlight
59.	the great wild forest
60.	the verdant walls of the forest
61.	the heavy frame of the forest
62.	in the midst of a large and thick forest
63.	the sun shone brightly between the trunks of the trees into the dark green of the forest
64.	the cold in the shades of this singular forest was intense
65.	a perfect forest of green trees
66.	the deep black forest
67.	like sunset glimmers in a shadowy forest
68.	a forest of hundred-foot pines
69.	a forest of thick trees that grew close together
70.	the lower terraces of the forest

71. a tender green forest
72. dense patches of lofty forest
73. a copse of lofty forest trees, sleeping in the melancholy moonlight
74. the green waves of the forest
75. the autumn forest
76. the dense redwood forest
77. the forest thick with woods
78. dense, untouched forest
79. the spendthrift richness of the forest foliage
80. solid forest walls
81. stretch upon stretch of almost unbroken forest
82. the dismal line of black forest
83. a dark, gloomy forest
84. patches of forest here and there
85. the vast expanse of the forest country
86. the barrier of forest
87. the forest below had a black and forbidding face
88. great wastes of forest

LS3-14 (LANDSCAPES - GROVE)

1. it was a perfect grove where bright gleaming berries glistened everywhere
2. high and strong trees formed the outer margin of the grove
3. the sycamores of the grove, make slow inclinations to the just-awakening air
4. the gloomy grove
5. in a sacred grove
6. a pleasant grove of tall and stately trees
7. grove stretches along the margin of the water
8. an ancient grove which had never been profaned by the axe
9. under a grove of olive-trees on the border of a rivulet

10. a blooming wilderness of grove and garden
11. a spruce grove over the hill
12. grassy bank beside the thick fir grove
13. a thick shady grove
14. a beautiful grove of trees grew up and overshadowed the place
15. amid the foliage of the bosky grove
16. a luxurious grove in the heart of the vale
17. a well-watered grove, with shady alleys to walk in
18. the hollows of the grove
19. a delightful grove of green leafy trees
20. the thick-leaved shadowy-soaring beech-tree grove
21. the grove had an architectural appearance
22. a gloomy grove of myrtle trees
23. in a dense grove
24. the flowering grove
25. the solemnity of a grove of ancient trees
26. the mournful stillness of the grove
27. a grove that keeps out the sunlight
28. a thick grove of palms
29. grove of gigantic cypresses fling their broad shadows over the land
30. a grove of wild mulberry trees
31. green-glooming twilight of the grove
32. a great grove of olive trees
33. a grove of lemon trees- cool, shady, hung with fruit
34. the noble grove of orange trees
35. that sunlit scene of grove
36. in a park-like grove
37. a beautiful grove dotted with huge boulders half embedded in the rich
38. loam
39. little grove of orange trees at the end of the garden
40. the road winding through a vast grove of silver trees

41. a grove of tall walnut-trees that shades one side of the valley
42. a fruitful orange grove of five thousand trees
43. grove of fragrant myrtle

LS3-15 (LANDSCAPES - TRACK)

1. was a hundred miles off the track
2. winter rains made the track heavy
3. the subterranean goose-track
4. far from the accustomed track of passing cars
5. right in the track of all the traffic
6. it was the original track laid out by the legions of the Empire
7. a track of some sort must have existed in very remote times
8. the ancient track of the lava is still open
9. had followed his accustomed track
10. was found to be the shortest track
11. six feet of the track that led to
12. they started to walk down the track before turning into the lane
13. took the rough track up through the wooded country
14. set off along the back track
15. the track wound along a hillside
16. where the hill-track failed
17. the track is rough but you can pick your way along it with care
18. the straight track, further on joined the highway
19. along the ridge ran a faint foot-track
20. track led over the hill
21. the wheel-track was little worn and even
22. the track that led through the forest
23. the double track turned sharp off and took the direction of
24. he went down the brick track

25. the wet, red track, already sticky with fallen leaves
26. the track went up the steep bank between the grass
27. the track they were following forked
28. a rough track leading to what proved a shallow ford
29. along the level track
30. a faintly marked cart-track
31. this sandy track
32. a side track in the forest
33. a narrow footway runs beside the track
34. the little track branched off
35. the foot track wound, half beaten, up to
36. the foot track, so dainty narrow, just like a sheep track
37. a single track, barely wide enough to receive the sleigh
38. along the track on the side of the mountain
39. a sinuous track
40. the main track was already cleared
41. along the track which ran parallel with the river
42. the track made off into a by-path through a piece of
     woodland
43. all vestige of the track was lost sight of

MS
MANMADE STRUCTURES

MS4-1 (MANMADE STRUCTURES - BRIDGES)

1. at the foot of a bridge
2. reached by the one-arched bridge
3. silent the crumbling bridge we cross
4. fantastic bridge
5. in a suspension bridge cable
6. the high corner-stones of the bridge
7. the south side of the bridge
8. on that perilous bridge
9. the temporary bridge

10. striking the innocent bridge
11. brave the unknown bridge
12. a small concrete bridge
13. the center arch of the bridge
14. the upper and lower pool below the bridge
15. through the triple arches of a bridge
16. crossed the ditch upon a plank bridge
17. across a broad bridge
18. huge bridge of planks laid upon eight ships chained together
19. the stone bridge
20. by a narrow plank-bridge
21. the elegant marble bridge
22. beyond the covered bridge
23. over the balustrades of the bridge
24. on the ice-bridge
25. sustain the floor of the bridge
26. a nook of the frame- work of the bridge
27. threw open an adjacent window of the bridge
28. the wooden bridge
29. old bridge and its fortified gateway
30. on the bridge that spanned
31. to the foot of a bridge
32. recesses which surmount the piers of the bridge
33. the ancient bridge
34. within a short distance of the bridge
35. the railing of the bridge
36. a bridge which had been
37. ascertained to be unsafe
38. a bridge amid our way
39. it was a shining bridge connecting two shining civilizations
40. a marble bridge
41. the form of a frail bridge over the abyss beneath
42. over which is a bridge that unites them

43. the canal at the castle bridge
44. that stupendous bridge
45. this portentous bridge
46. cross the river by a covered bridge
47. an iron bridge thrown across the water and shining with lights
48. the trembling bridge
49. down the slope of the bridge
50. by a simple bridge
51. the great history of the bridge
52. into the throng of the bridge
53. this bridge- a single broad span of stone with balustraded sides
54. mouth of the bridge
55. seated himself upon the stone ledge of the bridge
56. the stonework of the bridge
57. hung it over the parapet of the bridge
58. a bridge where through a brook runs down
59. fragments of a great bridge
60. on the rail of the old sheep-bridge
61. the swing bridge
62. to the green turf bridge
63. the glorious endless imperial bridge
64. the fallen bridge
65. the famous bridge
66. a very good bridge
67. a quaint old stone bridge
68. the lower bridge
69. the broken bridge
70. the beautiful bridge over the canal
71. the small plank bridge
72. the dull winter light over the town bridge
73. He crossed a long bridge over a river frozen solid
74. the railway bridge

75. an old, high, narrow bridge with pinnacles along the parapet
76. very primitive bridge
77. a wooden bridge
78. rendered the bridge unapproachable
79. led her near the fatal bridge
80. on the narrow bridge
81. walked over that beautiful monumental bridge
82. horrid wire bridge
83. the curve of the bridge
84. I looked at the magnificent bridge
85. the mighty bridge

MS4-2 (MANMADE STRUCTURES - DAM)

1. seemed like a movable dam
2. which no dam could contain
3. like a great dam
4. stopping the current with their little dam-dikes of mud
5. like an unnatural dam
6. making a beaver-dam
7. to dam the waters of the great lakes
8. like a pent-up dam when liberated
9. a hydroelectric dam
10. through the generators of a kilometer-high dam
11. thrown a dam obliquely across the Rhine
12. a dam composed of brushwood and stones
13. to completely hide the entrance by making a dam and thus causing the waters of the lake to rise
14. to establish a dam at the two openings made by the lake
15. to maintain the mill- dam
16. at one end of the pond was an earthen dam, planted with green willow bushes
17. it was opposed by a stone mill-dam
18. rocks jutting out into the sea formed a rugged dam

19. we built with stakes and stones
20. a kind of dam that raised the water sufficiently
21. brought with him from its tender dam
22. a shapely dam
23. it would probably essentially dam the widest river in the world
24. like an undermined dam
25. in thy unhallowed dam
26. a suckling dam
27. the sea formed a rugged dam
28. a faithful dam
29. your unhallowed dam
30. on that narrow dam amid the wagons and the cannon
31. over a strong dam

COLORS

C1 (CLEAR)

1. clear as crystal
2. invisible traces

C2 (DAY)

1. drear morning light
2. blaze of sunlight
3. full in the sunlight
4. dusk-lit
5. slanting amber light of late afternoon
6. gilded dawn
7. high noon light
8. the sun tormented the air
9. dawn painted the new day
10. bathed in a golden beam of sunlight
11. scorching sky
12. first light
13. soft where the sunlight reached
14. broad beam of sunlight
15. ghastly parody of daylight
16. the gray of dawn
17. burned with the divine brilliance of the heavens
18. golden sunbeam shaft
19. brilliantly dappled by the bright morning sunlight

C3 (LIGHT)

1. sunlight
2. bathed in a golden beam of sunlight
3. moonlight
4. artificial light

5. independent light   fantasy light
6. illuminated
7. pool of light
8. source of light
9. glow of tiny lights
10. irritating light
11. ultraviolet
12. flooded with light
13. unimaginable light
14. flash of light
15. shining light
16. seas of light
17. one solid blaze
18. drear morning light
19. ghastly gray light
20. blaze of sunlight
21. full in the sunlight
22. midnight moon
23. shadow rimmed with light
24. bright moon
25. merciless light
26. dusklit
27. a shaft of sunshine
28. slanting amber light of late afternoon
29. great gold swaths
30. baleful light
31. fitful light
32. gilded dawn
33. high noon light
34. burning sun
35. the sun tormented the air
36. a bead of icelight
37. thread of a moon
38. dawn painted the new day
39. scorching sky

40.   polarized light
41.   flash of light
42.   multitude of candles
43.   first light
44.   soft where the sunlight reached
45.   golden light of incredible purity
46.   oceans of flame
47.   specks of light
48.   broad beam of sunlight
49.   violet lightening
50.   a wavering wall of light
51.   ghastly parody of daylight
52.   the gray of dawn
53.   single beam of light
54.   brief illumination
55.   dim pools of light
56.   seriously moonlit
57.   sea of floating light
58.   burned with the divine brilliance of the heavens
59.   rosy light
60.   opalescent light
61.   a brilliant shaft of light
62.   brilliant discs of light
63.   golden sunbeam shaft
64.   jagged curtains of light
65.   glowed with an inner light
66.   brilliantly dappled by the bright morning sunlight
67.   illumined pallidly
68.   a great shaft of golden light
69.   a bright gloss of light
70.   a sudden blaze of light
71.   pure shimmering light
72.   a rectangle of stark sunshine
73.   full of dappled sunlight
74.   the very edge of a brilliant pool of light

75.   a fine starlit sky

C4 (SHINEY)

1.   shiny as black chintz
2.   glimmers
3.   illuminated
4.   silver blur   shimmering
5.   shining light
6.   sparkling glory
7.   gold gleam
8.   one solid blaze
9.   glinting
10.   achingly bright
11.   sweeping shimmer
12.   sparking on gold
13.   glittering showers
14.   distant glimmer
15.   metallic gleam
16.   shining water
17.   brightness flashing
18.   flashing signals
19.   iridescent
20.   refracted glare
21.   a bead of ice-light
22.   a fat spark
23.   auras like halos
24.   flash of light
25.   multitude of candles
26.   iridescent droplets
27.   shimmering field of
28.   diamond bright
29.   oceans of flame
30.   thread of flame
31.   specks of light

32. brief illumination
33. silvery sparkle
34. darkly brilliant
35. a brilliant shaft of light
36. shining like pearls
37. fairie fires
38. glowed like a cauldron of star-stuff
39. glowed with an inner light
40. glistened with a diamond sheen
41. a bright gloss of light
42. pure shimmering light

C5 (METALS)

1.   black gold
2.   bronze gold
3.   silvery gold
4.   tawny-gold
5.   silver blur
6.   gold gleam
7.   jeweled
8.   sparking on gold
9.   great gold swaths
10. a flurry of gold
11. metallic gleam
12. silver-white
13. red-gold
14. wafers of beaten gold
15. fingers of gold
16. platinum   golden splay
17. silver tipped
18. golden as wolf eyes
19. golden light of incredible purity
20. dull luster
21. frosted silver

22. silvery sheen
23. glassy silver sprawl
24. muted aluminal sheen
25. dull silver
26. iron gray

C6 (WHITE)

1. porcelain pale
2. fish belly white
3. powder white
4. a bleached bone
5. ivory
6. bone
7. pale as parchment
8. silver-white
9. stark white
10. alabaster
11. snow white
12. starkly white
13. multi-foliate white
14. like dirty white caps

C7 (NIGHT)

1. midnight moon
2. bright moon
3. dusk-lit
4. thread of a moon
5. twilight soft
6. seriously moonlit
7. burned with the divine brilliance of the heavens
8. dark of the moon
9. raven waning moon
10. moonless sky

11. turbulent sky
12. dusky
13. night mist
14. twilight soft
15. inky night
16. being gathered into the clutches of dusk
17. the sky began to deepen towards sunset
18. star-flecked dark
19. deeper in the darkness than any true night
20. rosy twilight
21. rosy mists of dusk
22. the full thrall of night

C8 (DARK)

1. cold darkness
2. unnaturally dark
3. dark mists
4. inky depths
5. dark of the moon
6. full dark
7. moonless sky
8. dusky
9. deeply darkened
10. the dark made a black circle
11. dusky colored
12. masses of dense black smoke
13. star-flecked dark
14. deeper in the darkness than any true night
15. grotto dark
16. the darkness shrank back into the corners
17. huge vaulted darkness
18. midnight velvet of the sky

C9 (SHADOWED)

1. long shadows
2. lengthening shadows
3. cloudy with shadow
4. plume of black gold
5. a patch of shade
6. dusky
7. chill shadows
8. a shadow time
9. lengthening shadows of afternoon
10. twilight soft
11. murky shadows
12. blue-black shadows
13. vast shadow-land
14. convoluted blackness

C10 (FOGGY)

1. dark mists
2. mist shrouded
3. cloudy with shadow
4. cloud touched
5. night mist
6. wrapped in a cottony curtain
7. rosy mists of dusk

C11 (DINGY)

1. like dirty white caps
2. murky shadows
3. dull silver

C12 (BLACK)

1. glassy volcanic rock

2. inky blackness
3. anthracite
4. currant black
5. obsidian black
6. olive black
7. jet black
8. like black satin
9. black as coal
10. black as a raven's wing
11. black gold
12. blackness
13. absolute blackness
14. inky depths
15. plume of black gold
16. the dark made a black circle
17. blue-black circles
18. masses of dense black smoke
19. nigritude
20. nigrosine
21. drop dead black
22. slice of black space
23. ebon
24. grim black
25. convoluted blackness
26. intense unreal blackness

C13 (BLUE)

1. darker than sapphires
2. violet
3. smoky blue
4. azure blue
5. as blue as the summer sky liquid blue
6. icy blue
7. winter blue

8. faded dust blue
9. wild sapphire
10. Nordic blue
11. Genetian blue
12. blue flame
13. mellow blue
14. faded blue
15. pale blue
16. bright blue
17. sapphire blue
18. grey-blue
19. blue-green
20. cool blue
21. deep blue
22. dark blue
23. steel blue
24. blue-black
25. chalcedonic (pale blue)
26. onyx
27. induline (dark blue)
28. violet
29. azure
30. glowing blue
31. blackening-blue
32. subtle aqua
33. ocean blue
34. sea-blue
35. peacock-blue
36. brilliant blue
37. china blue
38. a particular shade of electric blue
39. almost bright blue
40. soft blue
41. somehow too blue
42. a tender blue

43. blue of heaven's own tint
44. remarkably blue
45. cloudless blue
46. celestial blue
47. the blue void of space
48. a deep bright blue
49. vivid ultramarine blue
50. a conspicuous milky-blue tint
51. cobalt-blue
52. slaty-blue
53. rich metallic blue
54. iridescent, greenish-blue
55. evening blue
56. sage blue
57. a slight shade of blue
58. lapis-lazuli
59. blazing blue
60. darkly blue
61. deep well of blue
62. clear as blue jade
63. wan blue of the heaven
64. ether-blue
65. blue of the violet's eye
66. blue in never-ending shades and harmonies
67. pure Irish blue
68. like a blue vein on a girl's white wrist
69. a sickly blue
70. a very undecided blue
71. as blue as the great sea
72. of the usual blue
73. the blue gleam of the lovely gentian
74. ugly dead-blue
75. a dead enough blue
76. the brightest, loveliest blue that can be imagined
77. transparent blue

78. an exceedingly mild blue
79. a ghastly blue
80. sickly blue
81. weirdly blue
82. fine deep blue
83. stainless blue
84. sparklingly blue
85. blue as zinc
86. the blue of the equatorial heavens
87. a strange color of blue
88. peacock-blue
89. vicious blue-white
90. stark blue
91. tenderest blue of heaven
92. pellucid blue
93. a deep celestial blue
94. veiled azure
95. pale blue of the zenith
96. hyacinth blue
97. a profound, unfathomable blue
98. blue as bilberry
99. blue meridian skies
100. devil's blue
101. blue blandness
102. a hempen blue
103. eternal blue
104. satanic blue
105. turquoise blue
106. blue like a peacock's neck
107. indescribable blue of an autumn sky
108. an arrogant blue which goaded the nerves like a spur
109. powder blue
110. dusky blue
111. blue deeps of heaven
112. blue as the flame of burning sulfur

113. a peculiar blue radiance
114. misty blue of the distant hills
115. like blue fire
116. robin's-egg blue
117. blue as Copenhagen china
118. as blue as corn-flowers
119. the blue of the forget-me-not
120. blue as soft as periwinkle
121. a very vivid blue
122. molten blue
123. blue as the azure of the sea
124. fairy blue
125. a sorry blue
126. blue as autumn mist
127. livid blue
128. unclouded blue
129. fathomless tropic blue
130. smeary shade of blue
131. licorice blue
132. Teutonic blue
133. the pale blue of the deep waters
134. heaven's unmeasured blue
135. viking blue
136. blue as the sea in sunshine
137. mid-sea blue
138. densely blue
139. delicate blue shading into opal
140. an inconspicuous blue
141. agreeable blue tint
142. a lovely shade of blue
143. sky-like blue
144. shallow blue
145. violent blue
146. clean-colored blue
147. ghoulish blue

148. deep and sultry blue
149. as blue as a piece of clear sky
150. the blue of a sudden sulfur-blaze
151. hell's own blue tint
152. larkspur blue

C14 (RED)

1. the color of a fair sunset
2. deep auburn
3. rich red
4. red-gold
5. a fat spark
6. a lambent rosy glow
7. ultrared
8. rosy-red
9. prim rose
10. red campion (a European crimson flower)
11. redgold
12. crimson
13. violent red
14. a very dark red
15. blood red
16. scarlet
17. safranine (red synthetic dye)
18. brilliant scarlet
19. magenta
20. glowing red
21. carnelian (translucent reddish quartz)
22. vibrant rose
23. carmine
24. somber red
25. iridescent red
26. striking rose
27. beet red

28. flame color
29. deep-red
30. dull brick red
31. fiery red
32. flame-red poppies
33. cherry-red
34. blood-red
35. vermilion red
36. bright rusty red
37. feeble red
38. delicate rose-red
39. rud-red
40. first blush of red
41. red as a lobster
42. full-blooded red
43. saffron-red
44. decidedly red
45. plain red
46. red as carrots
47. red as a beet
48. passion-red
49. red as fire
50. wine-red
51. warm, rich red
52. red of early strawberries
53. as red as the sun's disk
54. lusty red
55. coppery red
56. so red one could only think of cherries
57. loathsomely red
58. red like flame
59. coral-red
60. an indomitable red
61. red as a crab
62. a brickish red

63. morning-red
64. red light of the harvest-moon
65. purplish-red
66. red as a peony
67. red as a lobster
68. touched with red
69. a dusky red
70. blood-red as sunset summer clouds
71. red by nature
72. clay-red
73. geranium's red
74. pomegranate red
75. burnt red
76. like blood-red mulberries
77. cold red of sunset in winter
78. red jade
79. rich Indian red
80. vermilion-red
81. red as arterial blood
82. lion red
83. like the red of a peach
84. fitful red
85. the reddest red of the foxfire
86. red as a turkey
87. a soft red like an apple-blossom
88. red as a moss-rose
89. red as ripe new blood
90. unnatural red like the painted face of a savage
91. crawfish red
92. swarthy red
93. redder than great fans of coral
94. royal red
95. cardinal red
96. red as glowing coals
97. florid red

98. showy red
99. red as a peony
100. red as a lump of raw meat
101. a shade too red
102. like a field of red clover in full bloom
103. red from excessive agitation
104. a quick red ran up
105. fiery and unusual red
106. sullen glare of red light
107. like red cinnamon drops
108. like big dark red plums
109. deep, velvety red
110. molten red
111. as red as the feet of the dove
112. Phoenician red
113. as red and polished as a ripe cherry
114. aggressively red
115. the choicest scarlet red
116. red as the bristles in an old pig's ears
117. clear unmatched red
118. lurid red
119. red like wine that one has been colored with water
120. a deep, red glow, as of iron in a furnace
121. red from cold
122. a guilty red
123. artificial red
124. dewy red
125. too much red
126. cheerful red
127. desperately red
128. a color of uniform red
129. dingy red
130. an unvarying red color
131. bright cardinal red
132. so startlingly red as to be a wonder

133. red as a live coal
134. peculiar red
135. blazing red
136. flamingo red
137. feverish red
138. excessively red
139. red-tinted
140. living red
141. a color like blood, to which we give the name of red
142. red is the most pervading of colors
143. a deep Indian red
144. a more beautiful red than vermilion
145. pure red
146. red as a drop of blood
147. hyacinth red
148. carmine-red
149. brownish red
150. alder berry red
151. pearly and red
152. dazzlingly red
153. orange-red
154. far too red

C15 (PINK)

1. rosy twilight
2. rosy mists of dusk
3. sea pink
4. delicate pink
5. vibrant rose
6. striking rose
7. startling pink

C16 (GREEN)

1. bottle green
2. green ice
3. polished jade
4. gray green
5. cool green
6. country green
7. green guilt
8. slate-green
9. moss green
10. turquoise
11. hazel-green
12. emerald green
13. green-gilt
14. golden green
15. livid green
16. moldy green
17. rich green
18. soft green
19. pine green
20. pea-green
21. greenish-white
22. subdued green
23. pale vitreous green
24. hostile green

C17 (YELLOW)

1. flaxen
2. bronze gold
3. silvery gold
4. tawny gold
5. buttercup yellow
6. ash blond
7. the color of field oats
8. the pale yellow of a field of grain

9. sandy
10. the color of warm honey
11. lemon-hued
12. wheat colored
13. golden as wolf eyes
14. very yellow
15. yellow gold
16. creamy pallor
17. blond as barley straw
18. marigold
19. primrose
20. honey-toned
21. sun-bleached yellow
22. deep shade of cream
23. orange-yellow
24. saffron (orange-yellow)
25. ochre (earthy yellow)
26. hot yellow
27. wan yellow
28. cheery yellow

C18 (BROWN)

1. tawny shade of brown
2. chocolate brown
3. coffee brown
4. amber fire
5. limpid brown
6. sun seared
7. mahogany
8. ultra-mahogany
9. brown as dried seaweed
10. roughly tanned
11. polished leather

12. fawn
13. nut brown
14. deep brown
15. sun-bleached brown
16. silvered brown
17. chocolate-colored
18. warm earth brown
19. warm brown
20. chestnut brown
21. ginger-colored (strong brown)
22. light brown
23. sober brown
24. red brown
25. brown as new-turned earth
26. dun brown

C19 (PURPLE)

1. swept with violet
2. mauve (deep purple)
3. violet
4. lilac
5. purple-hued
6. blackish purple
7. brilliant purple

C20 (ORANGE)

1. fox colored
2. the color of a fair sunset
3. tangerine
4. copper
5. saffron
6. evil orange
7. deep orange

8.	flame color
9.	fierce russet of a fox pelt

C21 (GRAY)

1.	the gray of thunderclouds
2.	the color of gun metal
3.	like glacial ice
4.	soot gray
5.	the gray of dawn
6.	steel gray
7.	ghastly gray
8.	lichen gray
9.	cool gray
10.	dove-grey
11.	grey-blue
12.	gray-brown
13.	grayish tinge
14.	sober gray
15.	chalcedonic (pale gray)
16.	onyx
17.	smooth gray
18.	grey of the purest melancholy
19.	concrete gray
20.	iron-gray

C22 (RAINBOW HUED)

1.	rainbow-hued bands
2.	auras like halos
3.	iridescent droplets
4.	diamond bright
5.	tasteful rainbows
6.	pattern of violent color
7.	opalescent light

8. shining like pearls
9. chaotic maelstrom of colors
10. swatches of multicolored energy
11. exquisite multicolored flame
12. glistened with a diamond sheen
13. had the aspect of an impossible gem
14. shimmering in all the hues of the rainbow
15. a vision of breathtakingly chaotic color
16. colors roared like mountain wind

C23 (COLOR)

1. a gaudy, cheerful mockery of color

EARTH VIEWS
INDEX

COLORS
INDEX

A note from Sybrina:

Once upon a time I wanted to be a writer more than anything in the world. I could tell stories with the best of them, so I just knew I could write well, too.

Funny thing about writing, though...it's nothing like telling a story. I bet you've noticed that, too. I'd even go as far as to bet there have been times...plenty of them, when you've been writing along just fine, then suddenly, you hit a brick wall over how to describe the simplest thing.
25 years ago, there wasn't anything much available other than Webster's Dictionary or Roget's Thesaurus and a couple of synonym and antonym books. So, I decided I'd start to put together what I was looking for, myself.

Those were the prehistoric days, before p.c.'s. Each bit of information I gathered was tediously placed behind index tabs in spiral notebooks...lots of notebooks and tons of tabs. It very quickly became a monstrous task. When I got my first computer, with Word Perfect's word "search and replace" features, I felt like I'd finally arrived in the 20th century but the best was yet to come. Word for Windows made cross-referencing all those phrases to all of their relevant categories a breeze.

Compiling this book has been a labor of love. Along the way, I have discovered my true writing skills lie, not in writing out my stories, but in organizing and categorizing information. Maybe someday, I'll actually have time to write my own great novel, but for now, I'm content in the knowledge that my work on Sybrina's Phrase Thesaurus has made it easier for other writers to get past their own brick walls. I hope you will enjoy reading the phrases in this tool as much as I have enjoyed compiling them.

Happy Writing! Visit www.sybrina.com to see other offerings.

Sybrina's Phrase
Thesaurus Series

Volume 1
Moving Parts – Part 1

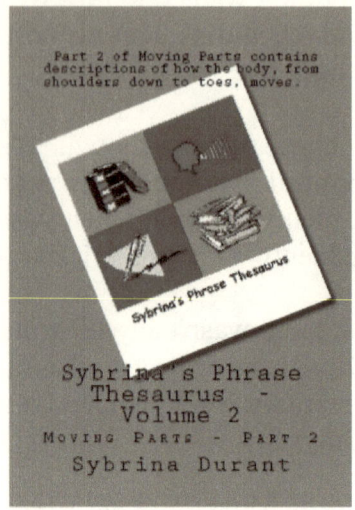

Volume 2
Moving Parts – Part 2

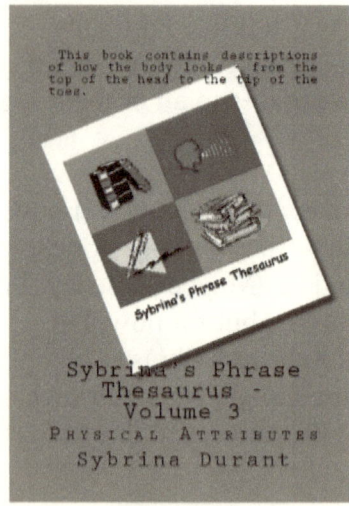

Volume 3
Physical Attributes

Volume 4
Earth Views

www.ingramcontent.com/pod-product-compliance
Lightning Source LLC
Chambersburg PA
CBHW020520290526
45786CB00002B/696